EAST-WEST TRADE

Other Titles in This Series

Nuclear Fuels Policy, Atlantic Council Nuclear Fuels Policy Working Group

The Future of the UN: A Strategy for Like-Minded Nations, Atlantic Council Working Group on the United Nations

Nuclear Fuel and American Foreign Policy: Multilateralization for Uranium Enrichment, Edward F. Wonder

The International Monetary System: Progress and Prospects, Atlantic Council Working Group on the International Monetary System

The Atlantic Council Policy Series

East-West Trade: Managing Encounter and Accommodation

The Atlantic Council Committee on East-West Trade

In the midst of the current debate over the effectiveness of détente, this book constitutes a unique and timely look at the question of implementation and reform in East-West trade. After placing the subject of East-West economic relations in its larger political framework, the Atlantic Council's Committee on East-West Trade examines some specific problem areas—the structures of the nonmarket economies, bilateral agreements, the General Agreement on Tariffs and Trade, multilateral negotiations, and financial mechanisms. The Committee assesses the effectiveness of these institutions and makes suggestions—among them, a controversial recommendation for the amendment of the Trade Act—for improvements that would facilitate mutually beneficial East-West trade.

The Atlantic Council of the United States is a bipartisan, nonprofit, citizens' organization concerned with the formulation of international policy. The Council suggests courses of action on problems and opportunities shared by the countries of the Atlantic Community—North America, Western Europe, Japan, Australia, and New Zealand—and seeks to promote the harmonious relations of these countries with socialist countries and the developing Third World.

EAST-WEST TRADE

Managing Encounter and Accommodation

The Atlantic Council Committee on East-West Trade

Lawrence C. McQuade, Chairman

An Atlantic Council Policy Paperback

Westview Press
Boulder, Colorado

The Atlantic Council Policy Series

Published 1977 in the United States of America by
Westview Press, Inc.
1898 Flatiron Court
Boulder, Colorado 80301
Frederick A. Praeger, Publisher and Editorial Director

Library of Congress Cataloging in Publication Data

Main entry under title:
East-West trade.

1. United States—Commerce—Europe, Eastern—Addresses, essays, lectures. 2. Europe, Eastern—Commerce—United States—Addresses, essays, lectures. 3. United States—Commercial policy—Addresses, essays, lectures. I. Atlantic Council of the United States.
HF3092.E2 382'.09171'301717 76-39928
ISBN 0-89158-215-0
ISBN 0-89158-216-9 pbk.

Printed and bound in the United States of America

$5.95

Contents

Tables and Figures

Foreword

East-West trade has become increasingly important to both the market and nonmarket economies. Although East-West exchanges have been limited for political and security reasons, they have been increasing on a substantial scale during recent years. Accordingly, the Atlantic Council has undertaken a study of the institutional framework of East-West commercial relations to determine how the United States can best pursue its trade opportunities while at the same time maintaining the capability to protect itself against unforeseen and perhaps undesirable developments.

This book is built upon more than six years of intensive work by the Atlantic Council on the subject of trade liberalization and reform. Early in 1974 it was agreed that many of the insights and much of the analysis and expertise which had previously been applied to problems of trade between industrial nations could be constructively utilized to scrutinize some of the problems involved in East-West commerce. Hence, a new Committee on East-West Trade was established by the council to undertake two objectives: first, to outline a reasonable East-West trade and commercial policy for the United States; and second, to examine in depth some of the technical, institutional questions involved in East-West trade reform. This book is the outcome of the committee's work.

The threefold purpose of this policy review and the accompanying special studies is (1) to examine how the United States can best go about increasing the volume of mutually advantageous trade with the Soviet Union and other Eastern European nations; (2) to analyze the adequacy of existing legislative and institutional arrangements relating to East-West trade; and (3) to make recommendations for policy changes.

The first part of the book (chapter 1) concerns the policy position .of the United States. It was the desire of the Committee on East-West Trade to look at some of the most important issues, such as technology transfer and market disruption, and to soundly anchor the entire exploration within the perspective of the political framework that encompasses East-West economic relations. The result includes some twenty-four specific recommendations summarizing the conclusions of the committee; these are listed at the end of chapter 1. The content of the policy review section is the sole responsibility of the East-West Trade Committee, members of which are listed immediately following the Preface. (Dissenting comments by members of the committee can be found in Annex A.)

The five special studies in Part 2 (chapters 2-6) examine some of the institutions which affect East-West trade (the structures of the nonmarket economies themselves, bilateral agreements, the General Agreement on Tariffs and Trade, multilateral trade negotiations, and financial mechanisms), with the objective of assessing their effectiveness and suggesting improvements which would facilitate mutually beneficial East-West trade.

The special studies are the responsibility of the individual authors, who have benefited from the advice and counsel of the East-West Trade Committee and independent experts too numerous to mention here, but to whom the authors express their thanks.

It is recognized that some of the recommendations and exposition contained in chapter 1 are based upon the special studies, while others are not. In those sections of chapter 1 not drawn directly from the special studies, the collective background and considerable experience of the committee was utilized as the resource for the material contained in those sections, as well as in arriving at all the recommendations set forth.

The Atlantic Council wishes to thank the members of the East-West Trade Committee who have served ably as joint rapporteurs for the policy section of the report, and the various authors of the special studies. Special thanks must go to the chairman, Lawrence C. McQuade, and to Willis C. Armstrong, a member of the committee, whose continued interest, contributions, guidance, and counsel benefited the project inestimably, as well as to John W. Evans and Jacques J. Reinstein, who were responsible for initiating the project and establishing a firm foundation for its development. The work of the committee has been aided by the sound comments and advice of the executive leadership of the council—particularly council Vice-Chairmen Theodore C. Achilles and W. Randolph Burgess, Director General Francis O. Wilcox, Deputy Director General Joseph W. Harned, and Assistant Director General Martha C. Finley—as well as by review of the council's Trade Policy Committee.

Financial support for the five special studies and the related activities of the East-West trade project was made available to the Atlantic Council under contract from the Bureau of East-West Trade of the U.S. Department of Commerce. (The Commerce Department's financial support does not necessarily imply endorsement by the department of the committee's findings, conclusions, and recommendations.)

The Atlantic Council is pleased to present this collective document in the belief that East-West trade relations is one of the many important topics which deserve study and public debate in order to achieve fundamental improvements in the overall international economic system.

As in all such collective efforts, not all the members of the committee or of the council agree completely with all its points. Some of us, including myself, have reservations on some aspects.

The arguments adduced for greater East-West trade by much of the American business and banking community, some of which are naturally reflected in this paper, flow from the simple commercial desire to do more business. So long as the Soviet government gives clear priority in its economic policies to achieving military superiority over the West, it would seem useful for Western governments, certainly our own, to judge East-West trade as a whole (not merely in the area of technology) in terms of its effect on the overall military capability of the Soviet Union.

The committee recognizes this in its recommendation 1, which reads:

> Any approach to East-West economic relations must recognize that politico-military considerations will be paramount in U.S. policy toward the USSR, and to a lesser degree in its policy toward other non-market economies. Economic policies can normally be expected to be supportive of and subordinate to political objectives when there is conflict between them.

Henry H. Fowler

Henry H. Fowler
Chairman of the Board
The Atlantic Council of the United States

Preface

The importance to the United States of our trade and other economic relations with the Soviet Union and Eastern Europe is modest in relation to our involvement in the international economy as a whole. However, this relationship has dimensions of consequence. Individual transactions can be of major importance to particular U.S. businesses. Each economy benefits from access to certain raw materials and technologies of the other. Poor harvests in the Soviet Union have, in some years, triggered major purchases of U.S. grains, with important effects on the U.S. farmer and consumer as well as the world grain market. Perhaps more significant, economic relations are a part of the overall set of relationships which the Western world maintains with Eastern Europe and particularly with the Soviet Union, and this total relationship is of central importance to world peace.

Integration of the international economic activities of the USSR and Eastern Europe with the rest of the international trading community is complicated because the former group of countries operates on a principle of state-owned enterprises and a centrally controlled economy. The setting of prices and allocation of goods and services does not rely primarily upon the free marketplace. These characteristics do not fit satisfactorily into the institutional structure by which the rest of the international trading community organizes and conducts its economic and commercial activities.

The Committee on East-West Trade has explored what practical steps might be taken to improve and make more systematic the conduct of commercial and business relationships between these nonmarket economies and the rest of the world. The problems are extremely difficult. Really good solutions must await substantial evolution in the political and economic settings of Eastern Europe and the USSR. Nevertheless, the committee has defined a substantial number of practical actions which could and should be usefully taken within the next few years to improve the ways in which these nonmarket economies and the market-oriented economies do business with each other.

Lawrence C. McQuade, Chairman
Trade Committee of the Atlantic
Council of the United States

Members of the Atlantic Council Committee on East-West Trade

Chairman

Hon. Lawrence C. McQuade: vice-president, W. R. Grace Company; former assistant secretary of commerce; director, Atlantic Council

Members

Hon. Willis C. Armstrong: former assistant secretary of state for economic affairs; president, U.S. Council, International Chamber of Commerce

Mr. Richard M. Brennan: director of international affairs, Union Carbide Corporation

Mr. M. Mark Earle: director, Center for Economic Policy Research, and assistant director, Strategic Studies Center, Stanford Research Institute

Mr. John W. Evans: former government official and U.S. representative to the General Agreement on Tariffs and Trade (GATT)

Professor Isaiah Frank: professor of international economics, School of Advanced International Studies, Johns Hopkins University; former deputy assistant secretary of state for economic affairs

Mr. James H. Giffen: president, Armco International

Mr. Steven Lazarus: international executive vice-president, Baxter Laboratories, Inc.

Hon. Harald B. Malmgren: consultant; former ambassador and deputy special representative for trade negotiations, Executive Office of the President; director, Atlantic Council

Hon. Stanley Metzger: professor of law, Georgetown University; former chairman, U.S. Tariff Commission

Hon. Christopher H. Phillips: president, National Committee on U.S.-China Relations

Hon. John B. Rehm: attorney, Washington; former general counsel, Office of the Special Representative for Trade Negotiations, Executive Office of the President

Hon. Seymour J. Rubin: executive director, American Society of International Law; former government official

Hon. Harold B. Scott: president, U.S.-USSR Trade and Economic Council; former assistant secretary of commerce and director, Overseas Private Investment Corporation

Mr. Kenneth Spang: vice-president, International Banking Group, First National City Bank; director, Atlantic Council

Mr. Stephen Stamas: vice-president, public affairs, Exxon Corporation

Hon. Philip H. Trezise: senior fellow, Brookings Institution; former ambassador to the OECD and assistant secretary of state for economic affairs; director, Atlantic Council

Atlantic Council, Ex-Officio

Hon. Theodore C. Achilles: former counselor of the State Department and ambassador; vice-chairman, Atlantic Council

Hon. W. Randolph Burgess: former undersecretary of the treasury, ambassador to NATO and OEEC; vice-chairman, Atlantic Council

Hon. Francis O. Wilcox: former executive director, Committee on the Organization of the Government for the Conduct of Foreign Policy; former assistant secretary of state; former chief of staff of the Senate Foreign Relations Committee; former dean of Johns Hopkins University School of Advanced International Studies; director general of the Atlantic Council

Mr. Joseph W. Harned: deputy director general, the Atlantic Council of the United States, and U.S. representative, the Atlantic Institute for International Affairs

Project Coordinator

Ms. Karen C. Taylor: Atlantic Council

Part 1
An East-West Trade Policy for the United States

1

Policy Review and Recommendations

The Political Framework for East-West Economic Relations

East-West economic relations are tied closely to the general political framework existing between the United States and the USSR. Within this framework, politico-military considerations clearly outweigh economic and commercial considerations in the United States' policy toward the USSR, and to a lesser degree in its policy toward the other socialist economies.[1] However, economic and commercial transactions between the United States and the socialist countries are a factor affecting the political atmosphere, and there is much to be gained from a reasonably stable economic relationship in which the socialist countries participate more widely in the general international system.

There are four points regarding the interrelationship between the general East-West political framework and the course of East-West commercial relations that are important to any serious analysis. The first is that, depending on the circumstances, the conscious manipulation of economic ties may well not be the most effective vehicle through which to secure political objectives. The United States' attempt to link the Trade Agreement of 1972 with the USSR to the USSR's emigration policy ended in failure, and as a result of this action the 1972 agreement has not yet entered into force—although the result may well have also been a consequence of the way the attempt was managed (on both the congressional and executive sides). Further, in dealing with the socialist countries, linkages between political goals and economic actions become complicated when U.S. congressional and executive policymakers cannot agree on what U.S. policy objectives are, what *can* effectively be linked with commercial concessions, to what extent, or how. More subtle use of the linkage idea has had its utility in East-West political maneuvers, but it is important to bear in mind that the growth and strength, and hence the potential utility, of the economic relationship can be stunted by an atmosphere of too much discontinuity in government policies, rules, and practices.

A second relevant aspect of the political framework is the importance of differentiating between the Soviet Union and each of the socialist countries of Eastern Europe. Despite their common characteristics as socialist states with nonmarket economies and inconvertible currencies, they have considerable diversity in their political and economic systems. Many economic reforms have been undertaken in these nations—Hungary has led the way in the decentralization of its foreign trading organizations, Poland in recognizing the importance of private initiative in agriculture and in seeking industrial cooperation agreements, and Romania in developing its foreign trade policy independent of the Soviet Union. Further, the Soviet Union, Czechoslovakia, the German Democratic Republic, and Bulgaria each maintain differing trade policies and methods.[2] The ability to grant most-favored-nation (MFN) status and negotiate trade concessions in response to economic changes within these countries has been extremely limited because of the tendency to view negotiations with the Soviet Union, in many ways atypical, as the model for relations with all the socialist countries.

A third point is the tendency in some quarters to overvalue the necessity for the socialist economies to import advanced technology from the United States. This unrealistic assumption may have caused us to overstate our political position, and as a result may have also weakened the United States' competitive position commercially vis-à-vis other advanced Western countries. The socialist economies have, to some, differing degrees, the capability to develop or obtain advanced technology from each other or to import it from a dozen industrialized market economies.

A final point in evaluating the East-West economic relationship is that both sides should avoid overestimating its relative importance to their respective economies. For example, in 1974 trade with the nonmarket economies constituted 1.76 percent of total U.S. world trade. In the same year, Soviet trade with the industrialized West represented 30.5 percent of its total foreign trade. In both instances, however, the value of trade between East and West remained minuscule in proportion to their respective GNPs. Numerical aggregates can obscure the importance of certain key items such as particular U.S. technologies, minerals like platinum, palladium, or chrome in which the USSR has a major share of limited world supplies, or American grain in times of poor harvests in the Soviet Union. Nevertheless, despite clear-cut advantages to each nation arising out of the commercial and trading relationship, an economic relationship of such a limited nature should not be expected to be of sufficient weight to enable the United States to negotiate major political concessions from the Soviet Union, or vice versa.

In a world of increasing interdependence—economic, scientific, and technological—East-West trade and commerce is growing and will continue to grow. A trend on the part of socialist countries toward greater use of economic incentives in planning and management is clearly visible. This is likely to continue. At the same time, there is some evidence that the United States and other market-oriented societies may adjust their international trading institutions somewhat to facilitate participation in international trade by the nonmarket economies on a more normalized and regularized basis. However, despite the fact that East-West economic relations may become politically or economically more desirable, they will remain of marginal importance to the United States and the USSR. This is less true for the socialist countries of Eastern Europe, with their long-standing trade patterns with Western Europe.

Each side has strengths in such areas as material and technical resources, research and development, and planning and management techniques. There are areas in which these strengths can combine to mutual advantage. In other areas, these may conflict. The optimal level of East-West trade may depend on the identification of competitive and complementary capabilities.

Policy Options

In its approach to East-West commercial relations, the United States has a range of general policy options. We could, for example—

1. follow a policy of virtually complete embargo;
2. maintain our current posture—that is, retain the current legislative and policy practices which define and limit the character of our dealings with the nonmarket economies;
3. attempt to eliminate some of the discriminatory trade practices which unnecessarily inhibit our trade with the nonmarket economies and evolve a responsible, but less discriminatory, credit policy;
4. combine this third option with institutional changes to facilitate mutually beneficial East-West commerce.

The Committee on East-West Trade favors the last option as a coherent goal meriting support from the president, the Congress and the American public. The policy recommendations of this committee include, among others, the following major items:[3]

1. Revision of the Trade Act and Export-Import Bank Amendments of 1974 to remove the emigration provisions and to give the president the discretion to extend MFN status and credits in exchange for reasonable commercial concessions.
2. Repeal of Section 406 of the 1974 Trade Act and reliance on protection against market disruption from nonmarket imports through the use of the strengthened

general escape clause as provided in Section 201 of the 1974 Trade Act.

3. Efforts to amend the antidumping and countervailing duty statutes to render them inapplicable to nonmarket economies.
4. Maintenance of current antitrust regulations, despite the alleged difficulties they create for American businesses.
5. Active encouragement of increased U.S. participation in nonmarket-country fossil fuel projects where competitively justifiable in security and economic terms.
6. Participation by the USSR and other nonmarket economies in a world food reserve system and, failing that, exclusion from the world food reserve system.
7. Judgments on questions of nonmarket-country participation in world economic institutions (International Monetary Fund, World Bank, General Agreement on Tariffs and Trade, the Tokyo Round of Multilateral Trade Negotiations) on the merits of each case and compatibility with U.S. interests.
8. Encouragement of the increased use of modern and effective commercial banking practices as the role of financing increases in importance.
9. Discussions among the Western nations on a common policy toward the nonmarket economies through the use of a model pattern for East-West bilateral trade agreements.

Structural Economic Differences between Market and Nonmarket Economies

One of the most apparent problems in the operation of the East-West commercial relationship is the basic structural difference in the way the two systems organize their economic activities. For this reason it is difficult to know when a trade-off between the two systems, such as a tariff reduction by a Western nation for a tariff reduction by a nonmarket economy, achieves genuine reciprocity. Several major characteristics of the socialist nonmarket foreign trade system set it apart from the normal trade relations between market economies.[4] These are the state monopoly of foreign trade, the planned nature of foreign trade, the nonconvertibility of currencies, and the treatment of much economic information as a state secret.

Foreign trade organizations and state-owned enterprises in nonmarket economies function differently from Western enterprises. The managers have different motivations and different day-to-day work habits than the businessman of the market-oriented world. Time horizons are different. "Profit" objectives are differently defined.

The state-owned enterprise does not face Western-style competition, Securities and Exchange Commission requirements, the gauntlet of quarterly earnings reports, stockholders' meetings and suits, or wide-ranging press and securities analysts' inquiries. The socialist state often assists its business enterprises in the management of individual transactions, supplies information as well as economic service or support, and even more important, will either guarantee them a market or accept the economic cost of accumulating a surplus. The socialist foreign trade entity can, if the state deems it advisable on political or other grounds, take commercial actions which ignore costs and the need to meet cost requirements. (Indeed, a major weakness of nonmarket economies is the difficulty or impossibility of accurately measuring cost for their own purposes.)

It would be useful in accommodating some of these structural differences if the nonmarket countries could continue to improve access to their markets and increase the amount and quality of information about their economies, both at the state planning level and at the enterprise level. Direct contact with end users should be encouraged in governmental discussions with the Ministries of Foreign Trade and those individuals having technical and commercial responsibilities in the relevant operating ministries. Although changes in these areas are taking place, the pace of substantive improvement is slow.

Mutually beneficial economic interaction between the two systems should allow both the Western market economies and the nonmarket economies to draw economic benefits from the interchange of goods, services, investment and management activities, technology, and knowledge generally. In spite of the differences between the market and nonmarket economies, the law of comparative advantage should allow both to benefit from an increasing flow of East-West trade and commerce.

Policy Issues

The Trade Act of 1974

The Trade Act of 1974 set certain political conditions relating to freedom of emigration as one of the prerequisites for the granting of most-favored-nation (MFN) treatment.[5] The emigration provisions were an effort to link political concessions to the normalization of trade relations. Moreover, the emigration waiver imposed short-term review periods (eighteen months for the first review and twelve months for each successive review thereafter) upon any bilateral trade agreement which might be negotiated to grant a socialist country MFN treatment. Continued extension of MFN status and credits to a nonmarket country with which a bilateral trade agreement has been negotiated is thus dependent on periodic approval given by both houses of the U.S. Congress to a recommendation by the president, based on his finding that the emigration policies of that country are satisfactory. Such provisions impose considerable limitations on the development of long-term, stable, and beneficial economic relationships.

The existence of these restrictive emigration provisions, therefore, makes it very difficult to negotiate bilateral agreements with the nonmarket economies that take adequate account of the economic interests of the United States as provided in other sections of the Trade Act. The goals of the act, which included "to open up market opportunities for United States commerce in nonmarket economies," have not been achieved, nor has emigration from the USSR been demonstrably facilitated. Quite properly the Trade Act takes into account broader aspects of policy, including human rights, but it is now desirable to move ahead in a practical way to advance both U.S. humanitarian and economic objectives.

The Trade Act of 1974 should be amended to remove the emigration provisions and to make explicit the right of the president to extend MFN treatment in exchange for reasonable commercial concessions. This would permit the negotiation of bilateral trade agreements and the normalization of U.S. relations with those East European countries that do not currently enjoy MFN status (Hungary, Bulgaria, Czechoslovakia, the USSR, and the German Democratic Republic).

The amended legislation should allow the U.S.-Soviet Trade Agreement of 1972 to enter into force or to be renegotiated. The removal of the psychological stigma of non-MFN status would remove an element of instability in U.S.-Soviet commercial relations, and permit the normalization and long-term expansion of two-way trade. It would also enable the United States to receive final payment in settlement of the lend-lease account, outstanding since 1945.

It would also be desirable to amend the Trade Act to revise the provisions which overturned the negotiated settlement of Czechoslovakian obligations in return for Czech gold held in the United States. In the Trade Act, Congress rejected the negotiated settlement and ordered a new negotiation under nonnegotiable conditions. This issue must be resolved before any consideration of MFN status with Czechoslovakia can be undertaken.

Amendment of the Trade Act requires that the Congress and the executive branch reach a compromise resulting in a more effective working relationship between them on matters relating to East-West trade and the general political framework of East-West relations.

The Export-Import Bank Amendments of 1974

The Export-Import Bank Amendments of 1974 (as well as the Trade Act of 1974) impose certain limitations on the

Eximbank financing of transactions with communist countries and also single out the USSR for more stringent limitations than are applied to other foreign borrowers.[6] Support for these limitations stems from three different points of view. One is simple distrust of the USSR and opposition to the extension of favorable government credit terms to communist buyers. Another is concern because the USSR is the world's second largest economy and U.S.-backed Eximbank credits could be disproportionately allocated to the USSR, especially if the huge gas projects under discussion between U.S. and European businessmen and the USSR should be financed by Eximbank. The third perspective views Eximbank loans at preferred rates to *any* industrialized country as unwarranted and as an inducement to a credit race by the Western industrialized countries. This last argument strikes at the very heart of Eximbank operations worldwide and does not apply exclusively to the USSR and other nonmarket economies.

In the absence of an effective worldwide agreement to refrain from preferential financing for exports to developed countries, however, this argument, as well as the others, becomes moot. In fact, competitor nations actively solicit Soviet and other Eastern European business through their government export credit programs (with the exception of West Germany, which offers credit guarantees but does not offer credits below prevailing market rates), thus rendering their products more competitive with U.S. offerings than might otherwise be the case.[7]

The Eximbank legislation also imposes a subceiling on credits to Soviet energy projects. However, the scope of many of the Soviet energy projects is so great that Eximbank resources are clearly inadequate, apart from any particular restrictions. Further, the problem of competitive pricing for Siberian gas might, in the normal course of evaluating a loan application, have led on its own merits to a refusal of Eximbank participation in the Siberian projects. Thus, the special subceiling contained in the Eximbank legislation on credits to energy development projects in the USSR is unwarranted on its merits, as well as being an obstacle to trade.

The committee believes the president should be given authority to treat Eximbank loans to the USSR and other Eastern European countries in a nondiscriminatory way. The existing mandatory discrimination causes many projects or transactions which might be handled from the United States to be carried out from Europe—often by a European subsidiary of a U.S. company—with European government-backed credit and the resultant loss of business and employment to the U.S. economy. Projects from nonmarket economies should be evaluated by the same criteria of creditworthiness as projects from market economies, i.e., repayment history, economic return on the loan, balance-of-payments data, and ability to repay as affected by government guarantees.

If, in order to protect the economic security of the United States, it is felt necessary to limit the risk of Soviet default, then a specific percentage of the total Eximbank loan portfolio could be established as an upper limit on financing for the Soviet Union, much as the legal lending limits today prohibit banks from lending over 10 percent of their funds to a single borrower. In order to give both the Congress and the executive branch sufficient flexibility to review such lending activity in terms of the general national interest, the actual percentage figure allocated for Soviet borrowing could be reevaluated periodically. Although it still provides for special treatment of Soviet loan applications, this procedure could be properly regarded as a nonprejudicial exercise of prudent portfolio management practice.

Finally, the U.S. executive branch should continue to seek the repeal of the Johnson Debt Default Act. This act was designed to prevent sales of securities in the United States or loans to foreign governments, other than renewals or adjustments, while the foreign government in question was in default on its obligations to the United States. The act is imprecise and therefore subject to a range of interpretation by the executive branch and the business community. There is little evidence that it has been useful in debt collection. Further, it precludes long-term lending and raises questions about participation in loans to large-scale projects, both of which are of considerable interest to the United States. The act should be repealed.

Export Controls and Technology Transfer

There is continuing Western concern that commercial transfers of technology not augment the military or strategic capabilities of the Soviet Union and the other nonmarket economies. On one extreme it is argued that transferred technology may permit the Soviet Union and the other socialist countries to divert internal resources to their military establishments. According to this argument, technology should not be transferred since it might ultimately contribute to their military capability.

On the other extreme, it is argued that U.S. companies should be permitted to maximize commercial returns on their technology (and the attendant employment and balance-of-payments benefits to the U.S. economy) by aggressively developing Soviet and East European markets for technology. This argument recognizes that this market is now in part being served by firms in Western Europe and Japan (including competitors as well as resident U.S. subsidiaries and licensees) which are the recipients of commensurate balance-of-payments and employment benefits.

In any case, it should be recognized that the West typically sells the East "used" technology. This means that the West sells current technology while the next generation of development is moving through the laboratory and is about to make the current state of the art obsolete in any event. Thus an extra advantage to the West stems from what might be called the salvage value of the technology. These arguments have some validity, but they are insufficient to justify an uninhibited technology transfer policy.

The U.S. government must continue its security export controls on both goods and technology as they apply to socialist countries. The policy set out in the 1972 amendments to the Export Administration Act of 1969 to keep U.S.-controlled items reasonably in line with items controlled by the Coordinating Committee (COCOM)[8] is a sound policy which merits continuance.

Technology control policy and practice require the advice of objective, technically trained, expert opinion.[9] Under the existing system, the Department of Commerce receives such advice from seven technical advisory committees including those relating to computers (mainframe), peripheral equipment, semiconductors, semiconductor manufacture and test equipment, machine tools, aerospace, and instrumentation. These committees, established pursuant to the Export Administration Act of 1969, consist of representatives of industry, government, and the scientific research community who are qualified to provide guidance on technical issues related to export control policies. At the same time, the Department of Commerce regularly taps existing areas of special expertise, including the National Bureau of Standards and the National Science Foundation, for technical assistance in these matters. It is important that these relationships continue.

A second objective should be to insure prompt decisions on export license applications. A protracted delay in a decision is in effect a pocket veto and is unfair to the American exporter. The efforts of the Department of Commerce to meet deadlines for decisions established under the 1974 Export Administration Act have produced concrete results in terms of reducing processing time for license applications, and these efforts should continue.

In order to promote the stability essential to a productive commercial relationship, the great majority of license applications are and should continue to be treated on a technical and nonpolitical basis. However, it is a fact of life, that, in those rare cases where overwhelming political or security reasons warrant either granting or denying a license, the ultimate decision rests with the president. Nevertheless, it is desirable to keep these cases to a minimum, and the reasons for treating specific cases in this exceptional fashion should be clearly stated.

Another element which would promote stability would be some form of satisfactory systematic review of technology transfer policy with the appropriate Congressional leaders, *in addition to* the dialogue associated with periodic review of the Export Administration Act legislation. Congress has been less than unified or consistent in its attitude regarding technology transfer to the Soviet Union and Eastern Europe. A continuous working relationship between the executive branch and the Congress on this issue could lead to better understanding and greater consistency with regard to export control policy.

From time to time, it may also be useful to expand the current practice of informing and advising Soviet and other communist officials about specific export license applications. This should be done in such a way as not to reveal the details of the criteria being applied to the specific application, but to advise the potential importer of any problems which may be developing with regard to the intended use of the goods. The Soviet Union has stated that its policies can be adjusted at the highest levels, if it is advised in a timely fashion. In this limited number of unusual cases, the U.S. exporter's prospects for getting a license on a basis compatible with U.S. security considerations will be improved by such consultation. However, if a satisfactory resolution cannot be reached, the exporter may choose to withdaw the application rather than have it denied.

Finally, the U.S. government should press for expanded access to attractive Soviet and Eastern European technologies. The Soviets, for example, have amply demonstrated their capability to achieve specific advanced technological goals. The United States should encourage, under the 1972 Agreement on Cooperation in the Fields of Science and Technology, more direct access to the potential generators of Soviet technology. Second, U.S. industries should seek and receive more information about advanced or commercially attractive Soviet and other Eastern European technologies. In other words, technology transfer should be a two-way street.

Market Disruption

What economic conditions should exist in order to justify the imposition of special restrictions on imports from a nonmarket economy? What statutory authorities should be provided in order to impose such restrictions?

Section 406 of the Trade Act of 1974, which provides measures against market disruption, assumes that the general authority to deal with injurious imports—the escape clause—does not adequately cover imports from nonmarket economies. Section 406 therefore establishes less rigorous economic conditions for restricting such imports and more rigorous statutory authorities for doing so.[10]

But the assumption underlying Section 406 is not valid. The new and liberalized escape clause of the Trade Act of 1974 can effectively deal with injurious imports from either a market economy or a nonmarket economy. If it cannot be demonstrated that increased imports are a substantial cause or threat of serious injury to a domestic industry, then import restrictions would not be justified whatever the source of the imports. Accordingly, Section 406 should be repealed. By such action, another economically unnecessary discrimination against trade with nonmarket economies would be eliminated, without risk to the American economy.

Furthermore, provisions can be added to bilateral trade agreements which deal with market disruption, such as Annex 1 of the dormant U.S.-USSR Trade Agreement of October 1972.[11] In particular, Annex 1 provides that, after consultation, the Soviet government will limit exports to the United States of a certain product if the U.S. government advises that such exports "could cause, threaten or contribute to disruption of the [U.S.] market." Indeed, such provisions are required by the Trade Act of 1974, and repeal of Section 406 would not in any way affect the inclusion of such provisions in future bilateral agreements.

As for the U.S. antidumping and countervailing duty statutes, by their very purpose and nature they apply to the trade of market economies. The antidumping statute deals with the economic behavior of private companies in the marketplace. It assumes that an objective comparison can be made between the price of the export and either the home market price or the cost of production. In the case of a nonmarket economy, such limited data as is available on the home market price or the cost of production is generally considered to be unrealistic. The problem is one of comparing costs according to a meaningful yardstick. In the absence of adequate data, the antidumping statute provides that the comparison must be made on the basis of similar products from a third country where the price can be determined (a market economy)—a principle which is admittedly arbitrary, difficult and perhaps impossible to apply in a satisfactory way.

The countervailing duty statute is equally difficult to reconcile with nonmarket practices and structures. It assumes a clear distinction between the government, on the one hand, and private companies, on the other hand. If the former subsidizes the latter, then countervailing duties are in order. But how can such a scheme be rationally applied where all exporting activities are state monopolies and where both production and trade information are limited?

In short, the antidumping and countervailing duty statues of the United States should be amended to render them inapplicable to imports from nonmarket economies.[12] Any necessary import protection can be provided under the revised safeguard clause of the Trade Act of 1974, and can be supplemented if necessary by market disruption provisions of bilateral trade agreements. However, to suggest a reopening of the legislative argument on antidumping and countervailing duty law is to run the risk of subjecting all the provisions of these general statutes to amendment in a protectionist direction.

Antitrust

In dealing with socialist countries, particularly the Soviet Union, U.S. companies sometimes consider themselves to be at a serious disadvantage. Soviet proposals are often of such a magnitude and involve such a substantial degree of risk that no single private company is willing to assume the full burden and responsibility for such a contract. Further, it is believed that foreign competitors of U.S. companies share bidding information and reach prior agreement as to quoted prices, to the disadvantage of U.S. companies. And, of course, socialist countries can use a range of tactics available to monopoly buyers to obtain favorable terms.

For all these reasons it seems desirable to many in U.S. business circles that they be given the right to consort with respect to individual projects of finite duration. This right of consortium could possibly be achieved under the provisions of a revised Webb-Pomerene Act, or new legislation could be proposed.

It is not generally evident, however, that the apprehensions of U.S. businesses are fully warranted, given Soviet and Eastern European preference for the best of American technology. Further, it is not realistic to think that any suggestion to soften the impact of the antitrust laws would succeed. Current pressures for more stringent laws and regulations have considerable support. It does not seem practical, at this time, to suggest opening up the antitrust laws to benefit a rather small segment of U.S. business for the sake of increased opportunities in East-West trade, in itself a minor factor in the broad spectrum of U.S. commerce.

Energy and Raw Materials

Given the interdependence of the world energy economy, the more energy supplies developed within the nonmarket economies (for either external or internal use), the less pressure will be placed on other energy supplies.[13]

Whereas in the United States additional energy development depends on the discovery of new reserves, on greater utilization of nuclear energy, or on the development of coal gasification or solar power on a large scale, in the case of the Soviet Union it depends primarily on the exploitation of fields which are known to exist. Western Europe and Japan are currently attempting to arrange lending consortia to move Soviet energy projects along. The question is essentially one of how best to allocate limited capital, in member states of the Organization of Petroleum Exporting Countries (OPEC), the USSR, or other potential petroleum-producing areas. A balanced U.S. policy should look with favor on increased nonmarket-economy fossil fuel production as simply one of many areas that should be developed. As long as such a policy is part of a multifaceted approach (development of domestic supplies, development of alternative fuels, and energy conservation) to the energy problem, no undue reliance on the Soviet Union for energy supplies should result. In sum, there is no reason why sensible projects that probably will proceed should not proceed with U.S. involvement. Whether such involvement should include government credits is a matter to be decided on the merits of each specific case, rather than by a priori judgments such as those contained in the Eximbank legislation.

At the same time, any increased sale of fossil fuels could have an impact on the foreign exchange positions of the nonmarket economies. Hard currency indebtedness is a major impediment to the East's ability to import the goods it needs from the West.[14] As for the United States, the decision to import fossil fuels from the nonmarket economies is and should continue to be made on a strictly commercial basis, weighing the price of the fossil fuels, stability of supply, and quality considerations.

Soviet production of special strategically valuable metals—platinum, palladium, titanium, and chromium—should be viewed along much the same lines. However, despite the fact that the economic value of the nonferrous metals trade is relatively small, the special strategic significance of these nonferrous metals and their critical industrial, military, and high-technology applications may warrant a special policy of domestic stockpiling and the cultivation of alternative sources to a greater degree than is necessary in the case of fossil fuels.

Agriculture

Soviet large-scale purchases of wheat and other grains in 1972, 1973, and 1975 brought with them a disruptive effect on the U.S. and other Western economies. The problem posed for the United States and the West generally is twofold. First, the sporadic character of large-scale purchases from year to year makes judgments about the future most difficult. Second, the market operations are sudden, without adequate attention to the phasing of demand surges so as to minimize bottleneck problems (e.g., availability of rolling stock and port facilities) and market speculation and its attendant effects on prices in the home market.

These problems are more acute today than they would have been in previous decades because the United States no longer holds substantial stocks of grains, which act as a cushion against sudden waves of buying. Soviet grain activity does affect prices of food and market expectations in many parts of the world. Moreover, since the world market system is closely interconnected, with a few grain companies operating in many nations at the same time, a wheat purchase from Rotterdam may be European wheat which, when sold, is replaced by wheat from elsewhere.

The Soviet Union in particular operates through one agency, utilizing government-wide data, intelligence, and analysis of U.S. farm data as well as analysis of its own statistics. The situation for U.S. traders is markedly different. They operate in secrecy from each other, utilizing the U.S. data that is available, but with very limited knowledge about what is happening inside the Soviet Union.

The executive branch has wrestled with this problem in several ways. One method in use in late 1974 was to require informal preclearance by traders and by Soviet buyers of large-scale grain purchases. This was replaced by the negotiation of a bilateral U.S.-USSR grain agreement in October 1975, in which a lower limit of 6 million metric tons and a ceiling of 8 million metric tons (beyond which additional purchases would require prior consultation with the U.S. government) were established. Because of the potential to purchase additional U.S. wheat through the international market in Rotterdam, such a bilateral agreement is not as effective as it might first appear in attempting to moderate the impact of Soviet wheat purchases on domestic wheat prices, since it requires the cooperation of the European Community and other nations, which cannot be assured.

Related to these issues is a broader question of the commitment to build world food reserves, consequent to the World Food Conference in 1974. If some nations agree to pay for and build up reserves and others do not join in, there will be major problems. What happens to noncooperators in times of world grain shortage? If noncooperators get a "free ride," cooperators will have no incentive to continue to support food reserves. The Soviet Union must be a party to world food reserve arrangements, or else it must be treated as a residual buyer which can receive reserves only if the rest of the market can be satisfied within reasonable price boundaries. It would be most undesirable if the Soviet Union regarded the U.S.-USSR grain agreement as reason to opt out of any multilateral grain reserve negotiation, having already obtained a qualified export commitment from the United States. Looking to the future, the role of the USSR and other nonmarket economies should be viewed in the broad perspective of a multilateral agreement. Only a multilateral approach, which includes the major buyers and sellers, can hope to deal effectively with the problem.

Institutional Arrangements

Because of the structural differences between the two systems, it is important to examine some of the institutional arrangements which are applicable to East-West trade. A selected number of these arrangements are examined in the special studies (chapters 2-6). Those examined here are nonmarket-country participation in existing intergovernmental organizations, private financing mechanisms, and a proposal for a model bilateral agreement to be used as a pattern for the Western industrialized nations in their dealings with nonmarket economies.

Membership in Existing Institutions

IMF and IBRD. The question of whether or not to encourage increased participation by nonmarket economies in the International Monetary Fund (IMF) and the World Bank (IBRD) revolves around the nonmarket economies' ability to join these organizations without diluting the effectiveness of the bank and fund.[15]

Even if the nonmarket economies should accept the formal obligations of the IMF and IBRD system, their ability to carry out the intent of the obligations is questionable. To what degree this would dilute the effectiveness of these institutions is a debatable issue, since many member countries today do not fulfill all of the obligations.

One benefit of nonmarket-country participation would be that these nations would, at minimum, have to accept the rules and long-term objectives (such as general currency convertibility) of the IMF and IBRD system, which are designed to promote open economies. A more tangible benefit would be that these nations would have to comply with the substantial reporting obligations of the fund and the bank, thus providing increased economic information about the nonmarket economies for the use of member governments generally.

The Soviet Union has made it clear that IMF and IBRD membership is not an option it is considering for the foreseeable future. The question therefore reduces itself to membership by the Eastern European countries, whose share in the quotas and voting weight would be relatively small.

The fact that the international monetary system is in a state of rapid change, with the switch to flexible exchange rates and the elimination of a central role for gold, clouds these issues even further. Given this mixed picture, it is probably premature to consider encouraging increased participation by the nonmarket economies in the bank and the fund. Nevertheless, membership should remain an option open to those countries which are interested in and willing to undertake the important obligations involved.

The General Agreement on Tariffs and Trade (GATT). The GATT is essentially a multilateral contract and, as administered by the contracting parties, lacks both a strong executive and powers to enforce its rules. In contrast to the IMF and the IBRD, voting is on a one-country, one-vote basis. Its effectiveness depends on the confidence each contracting party has that the parties in general will interpret the GATT rules from a similar perspective and be guided by them. The provisions of the GATT have generally been interpreted in the context of the trading systems of most of the members, in which the major determinant of trade flows is marketplace competition and in which governmental intervention, when it occurs, is plainly visible. The tariff, as the principal instrument of such interventions, is subject to limitation by negotiation, and, under the GATT, may be supplemented by specified nontariff barriers only in special circumstances, which are themselves defined in the agreement.

When the commonly accepted interpretations of the GATT rules are weakened by serious departures from this standard trading system, the entire fabric of the contract is threatened. A contracting party that is tempted to ignore the rules in a particular case finds it easier to do so if such key concepts as nondiscrimination and unimpeded access to markets have lost their earlier force and have been successfully ignored by others. The special protocols under which some Eastern European countries have acceded to GATT have not overcome this dilemma but simply illustrate it.[16]

The provisions of the Trade Act of 1974 require bilateral agreements that are highly favorable to the United States and certainly more favorable than the provisions which could probably be negotiated in a protocol of accession to the GATT. The Trade Act also requires that MFN treatment can be granted only in a bilateral trade agreement consistent with the purposes of the act. This prevents the United States from entering into GATT relations with a nonmarket economy without first negotiating a bilateral trade agreement with that country. It should be U.S. policy to avoid the further dilution of the GATT contract in order to maintain its effectiveness in regulating trade among the Western industrialized nations. If other nonmarket countries do succeed in negotiating terms of accession, the United States should consider exercising its right, under Article XXXV of the agreement, to refrain from entering into GATT relations with them. GATT does not now, nor should it in the future, serve as the principal multilateral contract regulating trade relations between the market and nonmarket economies.

The Tokyo Round. Tariff negotiations, reduction of nontariff barriers, and the reform of GATT are currently being undertaken in the Tokyo Round of multilateral trade negotiations. Six nonmarket economies are participating in the multilateral negotiations.[17] The negotiators are attempting to work out special codes on nontariff barriers, such as the harmonization of industrial and other standards regulations. The nonmarket economies should be encouraged to participate in these special codes, provided that they can undertake obligations equivalent to those of the other signatories of the agreement. This may require special rules which compensate for the differences between market and nonmarket economies.

It is in the area of specific issues, rather than generalized obligations, that meaningful agreements can be made with the nonmarket-economy countries. As a case in point, the Western nations should encourage the Soviet Union and other nonmarket economies to join the proposed world food reserve plan discussed earlier. Such an approach allows specific issues to be resolved multilaterally, thereby usefully supplementing the current system of trade rules and subjecting the nonmarket economies gradually to common rules of behavior.

Financing East-West Economic Relations

In addition to the elimination of legal handicaps which burden the U.S. banking system (as discussed above), modern and effective commercial banking practices are needed to facilitate East-West trade.[18] Without private sector resourcefulness and inventiveness combined with firm government support for export financing, the ability of American business to compete effectively will be seriously jeopardized. Some international political scientists and economists have expressed concern regarding the extent of external indebtedness of Council for Mutual Economic Assistance (CMEA) countries, arguing that such indebtedness could give the borrowing countries "leverage" on the governments of Western lenders. In general, commercial bankers are content with CMEA-country debt levels and structure and have appetites for additional extensions of credit. They further denigrate the idea of "leverage," feeling that a default by any CMEA country would ruin the credit standing of these countries as a whole and thereby seriously restrict their future economic growth.

Innovative approaches by U.S. bankers to different financial markets will be required to finance exports to the Soviet Union, especially those of heavy equipment which take a long time to produce. U.S., Western European, and socialist banks must continue to be actively engaged in Euromarket transactions if the trade is to expand. U.S. commercial bankers should examine the merits of opening representative offices in the capitals of the nonmarket economies.[19] The question of whether socialist banks should establish representative offices in the United States should be considered in a framework of reciprocity.

Proposal for a Model Bilateral Agreement

Institutional differences between the nonmarket economies and the market economies are so fundamental that special criteria acceptable to both should be developed to improve the interface between the systems. Since the GATT does not provide a practical vehicle for giving institutional character to such an interface, a model bilateral agreement should be developed to deal with the unresolved issues inherent in a commercial and trade relationship between two economic systems built on such different premises.

East-West trade would be greatly facilitated if future bilateral agreements between nonmarket- and market-economy countries had a high degree of commonality with respect to basic issues where present institutions have no satisfactory answers. A model bilateral agreement employed by Western nations as the basis of their commercial relations with nonmarket economies is a possibility which should be examined. Such an agreement would contain provisions on as wide a variety of issues as could be negotiated, such as arbitration, industrial cooperation, safeguards against market disruption, and other forms of nontariff measures affecting trade and finance. The model bilateral agreement would not involve ratification by governments, but would in effect be an expression of intent to adhere to agreed principles. Such a model could first be developed in the Organization for Economic Cooperation and Development (OECD), where the major international, market-oriented trading countries are represented,[20] but to succeed, it would of course require consultation with the USSR and Eastern Europe.

The fact that the European Community has not yet renegotiated bilateral agreements with the Eastern European countries on behalf of all its members provides an especially opportune moment to pursue the idea of such a model. Widespread use of the same approach—or the same texts, if possible—would not only facilitate bilateral trade but would also foster a more multilateral approach to East-West trade. The purpose of such a model agreement would be to limit the disruptive effects of diverse national East-West trade policies and to provide an improved basis for participation by nonmarket-economy countries in the world economic system.

Ensuring Mutual Advantage

What general themes and problems have run throughout the preceding presentation? What role should government play to ensure that normal commercial relations with the nonmarket economies do not result in significant disturbance or disruption of the market systems of the West?

It has been seen that there is a need for improved U.S. government-industry cooperation; improved executive-congressional cooperation in the trade field; and improved government-to-government consultation and cooperation both between market and nonmarket countries as well as among the industrialized Western nations. Out of such an improved consultative process, one might eventually expect the development of new criteria which could guide business and governments alike. However, since the relationship between the East and the West is a fluid and evolutionary one, involving different systems which have different objectives, permanent rules and criteria to guide this process are difficult to develop at any one moment. Therefore, methods of ensuring mutual benefits must also be adaptive, based more upon procedural innovations and regular consultation than on the often too-rigid formulas of treaties and legislative language. A flexible approach is essential to ensure and protect the mutual benefits resulting from East-West commercial relations.

Conclusions and Recommendations

The U.S. government should have a coherent policy on East-West commercial relations on which the president and the Congress could agree and which would be supported by public consensus. To this end, the Atlantic Council's Committee on East-West Trade makes the following recommendations for the policy and practice of East-West trade and economic relations.

General Political Framework

1. Any approach to East-West economic relations must recognize that politico-military considerations will be paramount in U.S. policy toward the USSR, and to a lesser degree in its policy toward other nonmarket economies. Economic policies can normally be expected to be supportive of and subordinate to political objectives when there is conflict between them.

2. Within this framework, it is in the interest of the United States to increase commercial exchanges with the nonmarket economies, to promote the stability of the economic relationship, to be competitive with other OECD countries, and to induce the nonmarket economies to participate more widely in the general international economic system.

3. These goals, however, should not be pursued to the point where orderly trading relationships with the rest of the

world are impaired or our commitments to other nations are infringed.

Alleviating Structural Differences

4. The nonmarket countries should be encouraged to continue improving access to their markets as well as to economic data and planning information. Direct contact with end users should be encouraged as a useful supplement to negotiations with the ministries of foreign trade of the centrally planned economies. Although change has occurred in this area, the pace of substantive improvement should be quickened.

Trade Act of 1974

5. The executive branch should seek legislation which would amend the Trade Act of 1974 by removing the present emigration conditions which inappropriately link political and economic objectives and which impose short-term reevaluations of nonmarket-economy emigration practices inconsistent with a stable long-term economic relationship; and by making explicit the right of the president to extend MFN treatment in exchange for reasonable commercial concessions, and thus speed up the normalization of relations with Eastern Europe.

6. The amended legislation should be of such a nature as to permit the U.S.-USSR Trade Agreement of 1972 to enter into force, or to be renegotiated, so that the United States could benefit from this agreement as well as receive its remaining World War II lend-lease payments from the Soviet Union. It should also permit a formula under which the Czechoslovakian gold negotiation could move forward.

Eximbank and U.S. Banking Legislation

7. Authority should be given to the president to permit Eximbank loans to Eastern Europe and the Soviet Union to be made in a nondiscriminatory way, i.e., standard criteria of

creditworthiness should be used to evaluate each application. The Export-Import Bank legislation and the 1974 Trade Act should be amended so that the changes suggested above could be put into effect.

8. The United States should repeal the Johnson Debt Default Act which regulates loans and sales of securities to defaulted foreign governments. The act has little practical effect, but it contributes to uncertainty about lending to and doing business with the Soviet Union and certain other Eastern European countries, especially over the long term.

Export Control and Technology Transfer

9. The U.S. government must continue its security export controls as they apply to socialist countries. The reforms which have been undertaken to improve the technical quality and objectivity of advice on specific license applications through the use of technical advisory committees, as well as to speed up the processing of export license applications, should be continued and strengthened wherever possible.

10. The great majority of license applications are and should continue to be treated on a technical and nonpolitical basis. However, ultimate discretion on licensing of exports to Eastern Europe and the USSR must be left to the president.

11. Technology transfer policy should be frequently reviewed with appropriate congressional leaders, in addition to the dialogue associated with periodic review of the Export Administration Act legislation.

12. It would also be beneficial to make greater use of the current practice of informing and advising Soviet and other communist officials about the status of specific export license applications.

13. The U.S. government should press for expanded access to attractive Soviet and Eastern European technologies. The United States should encourage reverse technology transfer in two ways. First, it should encourage, under the existing scientific and technical agreements, more direct access to the potential Soviet generators of technology.

Second, U.S. industries should actively seek information about advanced, commercially attractive Soviet and other Eastern European technologies.

Market Disruption

14. Section 406 of the Trade Act of 1974, which applies special market disruption provisions to imports from "communist" countries, should be repealed, since it has no economic justification and simply constitutes another form of discrimination against trade with the nonmarket economies. The new and liberalized escape clause of the act is adequate to provide protection against injurious imports from any source—whether a market economy or a nonmarket economy.

15. The antidumping and countervailing duty statutes of the United States, by their purpose and operation, apply to the trade of market economies. These statutes should be amended so that current provisions are rendered inapplicable to imports from nonmarket economies. Such an amendment should avoid, if possible, opening up a legislative debate on other aspects, not related to the nonmarket economies, of the general antidumping and countervailing statutes.

Antitrust

16. No revisions of antitrust requirements seem warranted at this time, despite the alleged difficulties they create for American businesses dealing with the USSR.

Energy

17. Given the interdependence of the world energy economy, the more energy supplies developed within the nonmarket economies, the more alternatives for acquiring energy will exist. Increased sale of fossil fuels by the USSR and Eastern Europe could significantly enhance the foreign exchange positions of these countries. U.S. involvement in

sensible projects should not be unduly inhibited by legislation. The decision to import is and should continue to be made by U.S. companies and regulatory agencies on a commercial basis.

Raw Materials

18. Soviet production of special strategically valuable metals—platinum, palladium, titanium, and chromium—should be viewed along the same lines as indicated in recommendation 17 above, except that the strategic significance of these materials requires a policy of domestic stockpiling and the cultivation of alternative sources to a greater degree than is necessary in the case of fossil fuels.

Agriculture

19. Since the world market in grains is so closely interconnected, and large-scale Soviet purchases have affected world market prices drastically, the Western nations should strongly encourage the Soviet Union and other nonmarket economies to join the proposed world food reserve or be subject to discrimination by being excluded from it. Only this type of multilateral approach, which includes the major buyers and sellers, can hope to deal effectively with the problem.

Institutional Arrangements

20. The option of membership in the International Monetary Fund and the World Bank remains open to the nonmarket economy countries. Such membership could be useful insofar as the nonmarket economies could subscribe to the rules and long-term objectives of the IMF and IBRD system, and would agree to comply with the reporting obligations of the fund. However, it is unlikely that the Soviet Union is interested in membership in the near future.

21. In many instances factors which determine the nature, quantity, and source of imports into most nonmarket economies bear little resemblance to those with which the com-

mercial policy rules of the GATT were designed to deal. To change those rules to fit the realities of East-West trade under present conditions could only destroy their ability to preserve order in the trading relations among market economies. But to ignore the differences between economic systems and pretend that the nonmarket economies can comply with the existing provisions of the GATT would do even more serious damage.

The special protocols under which some Eastern European countries have acceded to GATT have not overcome this dilemma but simply illustrate it. Nor is there any reason to believe that a different multilateral institution with broad Eastern and Western membership would be any more successful.

The United States should shape its policies so as to avoid further debasement of the GATT rules and should preserve the ability to negotiate more favorable terms in bilateral agreements with the nonmarket economies. If those countries do succeed in negotiating terms of accession to the GATT, the United States should consider exercising its right, under Article XXXV of the agreement, to refrain from entering into GATT relations with them.

22. Nonmarket countries should be encouraged to participate in the special codes and agreements, such as the standards code, which may be negotiated in the multilateral trade negotiations in Geneva, provided that they can undertake obligations equivalent to those undertaken by other signatories of the special agreements. This may require special rules in each case, which compensate for the differences between market and nonmarket economies.

23. The role of finance in East-West trade has increased in importance. Modern and effective banking practices on the part of nonmarket countries should be encouraged to facilitate the growth of trade.

24. The OECD countries, to the extent possible, should have a common policy toward the nonmarket economies which would seek uniform standards on government credit extension, on arbitration, on industrial cooperation, on MFN treatment, on safeguards against market disruption,

and on other forms of nontariff measures affecting trade and finance. A model bilateral agreement or set of guidelines should be developed by the OECD countries that would attempt to formulate common positions on these issues. The model bilateral agreement would contain substantive provisions to serve as guidelines in negotiating bilateral agreements between nonmarket- and market-economy countries. The model would not be formally negotiated by governments but would consist of an expression of intent to adhere to the agreed practices to the extent possible. The purpose should be to limit the disruptive effects of diverse national East-West trade policies and to provide a sound basis for maximal participation in the world economic system by the nonmarket economies.

Annex A
Comments by Committee Members

On Countervailing and Antidumping Duties by John W. Evans

I am not able to accept the portions of the report that deal with the U.S. countervailing duty and antidumping statutes as they apply to imports from nonmarket economies (NMEs). The statement of the issue is misleading and the remedy proposed needs refining if it is to be equitable and workable.

To suggest that these statutes "by their purpose" are not applicable to the trade of NMEs seems to ignore their true purpose: namely, to provide a means for correcting the trade distortions that result from subsidies by governments or from differential pricing by producing or exporting enterprises. Both these causes of distortion exist in communist economies.

The problem of applying the statutes to imports from NMEs arises not because those countries do not subsidize or "dump," but because the facts required for determining the amount of the subsidy or the margin of dumping cannot be ascertained; to apply the statues it is necessary to resort to arbitrary decisions in place of objective measurement.

The panel's recommendation that the statutes be amended so as to exempt East-West trade would remove the problem of measurement but would create other problems. It is probably true that the revised "safeguard" clause of the Trade Act would meet the needs of domestic producers injured by imports of dumped or subsidized goods from NMEs. But, if so, this must also be true of imports from market economies. If the panel had recommended that the statutes be totally repealed and that the safeguard provision be the sole recourse, regardless of the source of the imports, it would at least have been consistent and would have preserved some symmetry in the treatment of imports from the two categories of country.

The asymmetry that the recommended action would

create is compounded by the fact that, under U.S. law, a petitioner for relief against subsidized imports is not required to show that a domestic industry is being injured by the imports. Under the panel's proposal the right to redress in the absence of injury would exist only if the imports come from market economies.

I agree that a way should be found to correct the anomaly of trying to force NME imports into the ill-fitting structure provided by the present statutes. But this should be accomplished without creating new forms of discrimination in the treatment of trade from different sources. At a minimum the legal exemption of NME trade from the statutes should await the equally desirable amendment of the countervailing duty statute to include an injury test—an amendment that would bring U.S. practice into full conformity with the rules of the GATT.

On Export Controls and Technology Transfer by Philip H. Trezise

If this is all technology controls are to amount to (i.e., COCOM-agreed items), there is hardly any need for the Export Controls and Technology Transfer section of this chapter. But once the controls go beyond the obvious things, somebody has to decide what we are trying to do. I am very doubtful that "expert" technical opinion is what is wanted. "Technology" is an extremely imprecise term in the security control context; from my own experience, it can mean anything that an interested agency wishes it to mean: a single machine, a system of organizing machines, a technique, a patent, even a blueprint for a minor piece of processing equipment. If you turn to the expert, he is more than likely going to say that of course items in his field are important. If they were not, why would he have bothered becoming an expert?

It does seem to me that the argument for technology controls must be found, if at all, in economic analysis. The basic premise, I should suppose, is that the communists stand to make extra big gains when they are able to buy Western technology, which Western sellers are ready to offer at market prices, although the communists would willingly pay much more if necessary. So there is, to use trade theory terminology, a large consumer's surplus for the communists to appropriate.

If this is the case for controls, and I am at a loss to see another, it has two serious flaws. The first is the implicit proposition that the owners of technology either do not understand the communist interest in their product or, if they do, cannot take advantage of their bargaining position. This hardly rings true. Technology is typically in the hands of large, sophisticated Western companies; it is, moreover, likely to be unique or at least highly differentiated, so that it is not sold in a textbook competitive market. Why one should assume that these sellers would not appropriate some or all of the presumed excess gain for themselves is not at all apparent.

The other flaw is that the logic of potential outsized gains from technology does not square with what we know of the East, or anyway the Soviet Union. All observers agree that the USSR is more proficient in advanced technology than in the production of consumer goods or food; this is of course consistent with the regime's emphasis on having enough or more than enough *high quality* military hardware, which depends in turn on a large industrial base. (We tend to forget that the USSR currently generates some $700 billion worth of goods and services.) Western technology in many fields may be better, but it is unlikely that it is generally so much better that the Moscow managers would, if need be, pay very high prices for it. If that is admitted, then the basic argument for controls becomes quite shaky.

In the circumstances—recognizing that, given the high political quotient of this subject, technology controls above COCOM levels will be continued for a while still—disputed cases ought to be given the benefit of an economic review. Estimates of the possible Eastern gains will always be imprecise, but advisory opinions from, say, the staff of the

Council of Economic Advisors would at least help to set thinking straight.

Part 2
East-West Trade Institutions

An Introduction to the Special Studies

Part 1 of this book has approached the problem of how to responsibly increase the mutual benefits of East-West commercial relations by making recommendations on policy and by seeking to define an optimum East-West commercial policy for the United States. A different method—used in Part 2—is to address the question of *how* the task can be accomplished, specifically by evaluating some of the tools available. The approach of the special studies which follow is therefore to examine a few select East-West trade institutions (the foreign trade structure of the nonmarket economies, bilateral trade and economic agreements, multilateral institutions—the GATT and multilateral trade negotiations—and the various financial instruments) in order to determine the role each of these plays, assess their effectiveness in promoting (or impeding) East-West trade, and suggest possible areas for improvement.

An investigation of the institutions affecting East-West trade is especially important because of the differences in the economic structures of market economies and nonmarket economies and the need to accommodate these differences so that exchange can take place and be mutually beneficial. Most international trade and commercial institutions in use today evolved during a period when market economies were the major traders, and these institutions are, of course, based on market-oriented premises. This is not to say that there is necessarily anything wrong with these institutions today. On the contrary, they are highly effective in dealing with the major bulk of international transactions. However, their effectiveness is not as consistently good when dealing with East-West commercial relations.

So the questions remain. What will work? What institutional improvements can be made? How can the structural economic differences be accommodated without damage to either system?

The first study, "The Organization and Conduct of East-West Trade by Nonmarket Economies," by Charles Movit, looks at the existing trade patterns and foreign trade structure of the nonmarket economies (NMEs) in order to determine how the NMEs trade, how this differs from Western trade behavior, and in what ways the NMEs are altering their own trade patterns.

The second paper, "The Role of Bilateral Agreements in East-West trade," by Karen Taylor, examines that useful—and often used—East-West instrument, the general trade and economic bilateral agreement, in order to explore in detail the variety of functions this instrument can fill and the types of issues it will often address.

The third paper, "GATT as a Framework for East-West Trade," by John Evans, discusses the most important Western multilateral trade institution, the General Agreement on Tariffs and Trade (GATT), and outlines the different ways NMEs have become members of the GATT. The purpose of this examination is to evaluate the feasibility of a multilateral approach to East-West trade at the current time and within the setting of the GATT.

The fourth paper, "The Tokyo Round and the Nonmarket Economies: A Focus on Nontariff Barriers," by Karen Taylor, examines the current ongoing multilateral trade negotiations in Geneva and their relevance to East-West trade issues. Special attention is paid to the question of nontariff barriers—a subject of increasing importance.

The final paper, "Financing United States Exports to the Soviet Union and Eastern Europe," by Alfred Wentworth, discusses some of the problems of providing the credits which keep trade flowing, and the financial restrictions which the United States has imposed upon its own ability to compete with other industrialized countries.

One conclusion that can be derived from these papers is that the problem of accommodating the structural economic differences is far from resolved. Some areas have witnessed greater success than others. Changes toward decentralization, more rational price structure, and participation in joint ventures by some NMEs have been beneficial changes, but are not yet in extensive use.

Financial institutions seem to have had the most success in adapting to nonmarket economic activity. This may be partly due to the fact that despite structural differences it is possible in an approximate way to measure profits, interest, and risk and to make an economic decision based on these criteria. Problems of exchange-rate control and currency convertibility have been circumvented to a significant extent, but not eliminated.

Traditional trade policy as usually established in bilateral agreements and multilateral obligations has not fared as well. Perhaps this is partially due to the fact that the structural differences have made it almost impossible to measure such key concepts as price, "fair trade practices," and reciprocity in trade relations. In the absence of agreement on basic principles, a multilateral approach is virtually impossible. Bilateral approaches are not precluded, however, and can be highly effective in many different areas, such as business facilitation and industrial cooperation. It may well be that the pattern of bilateral agreements which will emerge over the next ten years will establish some common principles that could eventually be multilateralized. This would be especially true if Western nations could agree among themselves about principles which should govern East-West trade. And, finally, the bilateral process can be supplemented by dealing with specific functional issues of immediate and widespread interest (for example, specific nontariff barriers) in individual multilateral agreements.

These special studies have one common rationale: the stabilization, harmonization, and steady expansion of East-West trade would be advanced and made more efficient by making it more subject to mutually agreed rules and institutions. Even without the improvement of major institutions, East-West trade will continue to grow. What the special studies attempt to suggest is how such growth might be better cultivated.

2

Organization and Conduct of East-West Trade by Nonmarket Economies

Charles H. Movit

It is evident that problems inherent in the interface between market and nonmarket economic systems will necessitate a unique approach on the part of both public and private sectors of the United States to ensure the development of commercial relations between the two systems on a viable basis. Also, the organization and conduct of trade by the socialist countries will determine their future interaction with the international monetary and trade systems.

In dealing with the nonmarket economies, this chapter distinguishes among three groups: the Soviet Union, Eastern Europe, and the People's Republic of China. "Eastern Europe" means the European members of the Council for Mutual Economic Assistance (CMEA or Comecon), that is, Poland, the German Democratic Republic (GDR), Czechoslovakia, Hungary, Romania, and Bulgaria.

In an analysis of the trade organizations of these nations, the Soviet Union can be regarded as an archetype of a strictly centralized nonmarket economy (NME), while the Eastern European nations represent varying degrees of departure from this basic model. Hungary, for example, as a result of a number of reforms instituted since 1968, represents the economy with the greatest degree of decentralization, both in industrial organization and in the conduct of international trade, among this group of NMEs. The trading systems of the NMEs and the implications of their domestic economic organization in effect present a number of nontariff barriers to exports from market economies. In turn, barriers to East-West trade are maintained by the market economies and significantly affect trade patterns.

Trade Patterns of the Nonmarket Economies

In terms of trade turnover, CMEA trade partners have from 1965 to 1973 been the most important for the USSR (with the exception of 1972) and for the Eastern European NMEs (with the exception of Romania, for which the CMEA share of trade dropped below 50 percent after 1967) (see table II-1). The major trade partners of the People's Republic of China (PRC), on the other hand, were industrialized Western countries and developing countries. Soviet and Eastern European trade accounted for less than 20 percent of the PRC's trade turnover in this same period.

The USSR is a major trade partner of the Eastern European NMEs, accounting for over 50 percent of Bulgaria's turnover in 1965-1975. Romania was least dependent on Soviet trade—it accounted for about 39 percent of Romania's trade turnover in 1965 and about 20 percent in 1973. In 1973, the six Eastern European nations accounted for 47.2 percent of the Soviet Union's exports and 52.8 percent of Soviet imports, a decline from 1965 respective shares of 55.7 and 58.0 percent.[1] Absolute figures on the distribution of Soviet and East European foreign trade and the trade of the United States with selected NMEs appear in tables II-2 and II-3.

These six Eastern European nations are, on balance, deficient in industrial and energy raw materials. Deliveries from the Soviet Union enable them to fill their annual needs. In a recent study for the Joint Economic Committee it is noted that more than one-half of Soviet exports to Eastern Europe consists of fuels, raw materials, and semimanufactures. These exports, in spite of shrinking exportable surpluses (especially in light of Soviet hard-currency needs), still account for over 90 percent of the crude oil, pig iron, and iron ore; about 75 percent of petroleum products, rolled

Table II-1
SHARES OF NME TRADE IN 1965 and 1973

	Bulgaria	Czechoslovakia	East Germany	Hungary	Poland	Romania	USSR	P.R. China
				NME EXPORTS				
Percentage shares:				1965				
To:								
U.S.	.2	1.0	.2	.1	3.0	.2	.5	0.0
Other I.W.[a]	13.3	13.8	7.2	16.9	23.3	23.4	17.1	28.9
USSR	52.2	37.9	42.7	34.8	23.7	39.7	—	9.8
Other E.E.[b]	23.4	29.3	27.8	31.0	35.1	23.6	55.7	6.8
				1973				
To:								
U.S.	.1	.6	.1	.4	2.8	1.5	1.0	1.3
Other I.W.	12.2	18.0	21.1	22.7	26.8	25.5	18.3	36.1
USSR	54.7	31.3	37.8	33.4	32.4	22.2	—	2.8
Other E.E.	21.5	32.7	31.4	30.6	25.4	22.8	47.2	6.2
				NME IMPORTS				
Percentage shares:				1965				
From:								
U.S.	.3	1.0	.5	.6	1.5	.6	.6	0.0
Other I.W.	20.5	12.9	9.2	17.3	17.6	28.0	19.3	39.4
USSR	50.0	35.7	42.9	36.4	31.1	37.7	—	13.0
Other E.E.	20.0	31.8	24.7	27.3	30.2	19.6	58.0	9.6
				1973				
From:								
U.S.	.2	1.2	.4	.8	4.5	3.3	5.7	13.9
Other I.W.	13.7	17.7	22.5	25.1	33.5	33.4	18.0	44.2
USSR	52.2	30.4	31.6	34.1	24.4	19.8	—	2.7
Other E.E.	24.2	33.2	29.6	26.0	24.7	20.0	52.8	6.0

Source: U.S. Department of Commerce
[a] I.W. = Industrialized West; [b] E.E. = Eastern Europe

Table II-2

DIRECTION OF SELECTED NME TRADE[a] (IN MILLIONS OF U.S. $)

	1965	1970	1973	1974 [b]
BULGARIA				
Exports Total	1,176	2,004	3,300	3,838
USSR	614	1,078	1,805	N.A.
Eastern Europe	275	431	670	N.A.
Developed West	156	260	403	N.A.
LDCs	86	156	306	N.A.
Imports Total	1,178	1,831	3,270	4,283
USSR	589	955	1,697	N.A.
Eastern Europe	236	372	753	N.A.
Developed West	242	324	459	N.A.
LDCs	61	112	223	N.A.
CZECHOSLOVAKIA				
Exports Total	2,689	3,792	5,917	7,364
USSR	1,023	1,222	1,874	2,109
Eastern Europe	789	1,213	1,963	2,206
Developed West	444	746	1,245	N.A.
LDCs	279	367	492	N.A.
Imports Total	2,673	3,695	5,997	7,543
USSR	955	1,209	1,798	2,058
Eastern Europe	851	1,123	1,964	2,372
Developed West	487	880	1,478	N.A.
LDCs	224	251	443	N.A.
EAST GERMANY [c]				
Exports Total	3,085	4,647	7,738	8,846
USSR	1,311	1,742	2,842	2,788
Eastern Europe	852	1,386	2,360	2,667
Developed West	631	1,058	1,915	2,603
LDCs	157	203	315	406
Imports Total	2,823	4,923	8,066	9,719
USSR	1,205	1,945	2,482	2,843
Eastern Europe	693	1,246	2,327	2,422
Developed West	638	1,350	2,735	3,492
LDCs	138	210	269	564
HUNGARY				
Exports Total	1,510	2,317	4,321	5,129
USSR	525	790	1,442	1,638
Eastern Europe	468	648	1,187	1,581
Developed West	322	558	1,059	N.A.
LDCs	130	208	451	N.A.
Imports Total	1,520	2,505	3,833	5,575
USSR	553	832	1,306	1,587
Eastern Europe	415	726	994	1,408
Developed West	381	623	1,108	N.A.
LDCs	121	233	309	N.A.
POLAND				
Exports Total	2,228	3,548	6,432	8,332
USSR	781	1,251	2,083	2,374
Eastern Europe	528	882	1,633	2,014

Table II-2 (cont'd.)	1965	1970	1973	1974[b]
Developed West	607	962	2,063	2,816
LDCs	212	319	466	873
Imports Total	2,340	3,608	7,862	10,471
USSR	728	1,361	1,916	2,353
Eastern Europe	706	1,000	1,943	2,035
Developed West	548	901	3,431	5,158
LDCs	245	233	369	671
ROMANIA				
Exports Total	1,102	1,851	3,738	4,935
USSR	438	529	829	N.A.
Eastern Europe	260	395	852	N.A.
Developed West	255	550	1,203	N.A.
LDCs	90	225	601	N.A.
Imports Total	1,077	1,960	3,505	5,060
USSR	406	501	694	N.A.
Eastern Europe	210	441	701	N.A.
Developed West	348	756	1,451	N.A.
LDCs	70	147	395	N.A.
USSR				
Exports Total	8,175	12,800	21,332	27,374
Including:				
Eastern Europe	4,553	6,758	9,964	11,491
China	191	25	136	143
Developed West	1,438	2,345	4,957	7,960
LDCs	1,181	2,088	4,070	4,773
Imports Total	8,058	11,732	20,984	24,861
Including:				
Eastern Europe	4,673	6,634	10,925	11,352
China	226	22	136	139
Developed West	1,601	2,780	6,124	7,979
LDCs	847	1,315	2,418	3,281
CHINA (PRC)[d]				
Exports Total	2,035	2,050	4,895	6,305
Including:				
Eastern Europe	95	165	305	345
USSR	225	20	135	140
Other Communist[e]	330	295	555	885
Developed West	575	675	1,805	2,735
LDCs	455	525	1,270	1,650
Hong Kong and Macao	355	370	825	910
Imports Total	1,845	2,240	4,975	7,400
Including:				
Eastern Europe	110	190	300	315
USSR	190	25	135	140
Other Communist[e]	215	165	270	475
Developed West	920	1,555	3,458	5,290
LDCs	405	300	805	1,160
Hong Kong and Macao	5	5	10	20

(a) Domestic currency converted to U.S. dollars at prevailing exchange rate, on F.O.B. basis (except Hungary-C.I.F.).
(b) Preliminary official statistics.
(c) On basis on West German Deutschemark/US $ exchange rate.
(d) For the PRC, exports are F.O.B., imports C.I.F.
(e) Includes Yugoslavia, Mongolia, Cuba, Albania, N. Korea, and N. Vietnam.
Source: *Handbook of Economic Statistics 1975*, Office of Economic Research Central Intelligence Agency, August 1975, pp. 54-59.

Table II-3
U.S. TRADE WITH SELECTED NMEs 1965-1975 (MILLIONS OF U.S. $)

	1965	1966	1967	1968	1969	1970	1971	1972	1973	1974	1975
U.S. EXPORTS TO:											
Bulgaria	4	4	4	4	5	15	4	4	6.5	22	29
Czechoslovakia	28	37	19	14	14	23	39	50	72	49	53
East Germany	13	25	26	29	32	33	25	18	28	21	17
Hungary	9	10	8	11	7	28	28	23	33	56	76
Poland	35	53	61	82	53	70	73	114	350	395	580
Romania	6	27	18	17	32	66	53	69	117	277	189
USSR	44	42	60	58	106	119	161	547	1190	612	1833
China	—	—	—	—	—	—	—	60	690	807	304
U.S. IMPORTS FROM:											
Bulgaria	2	3	3	4	2	2	3	3	4	8	20
Czechoslovakia	28	28	26	24	24	24	23	28	35	46	35
East Germany	7	8	6	6	8	9	10	10	11	14	11
Hungary	2	3	4	4	4	6	8	13	16	75	36
Poland	66	83	91	97	98	98	108	139	182	266	260
Romania	2	5	6	6	8	13	14	32	56	131	155
USSR	43	49	41	58	52	72	57	95	214	350	277
China	.5	.1	—	—	—	—	—	32	64	115	171

Sources: 1965-73
U.S. Department of Commerce, *Selected Trade and Economic Data of the Centrally Planned Economies*, May 1975.

1974-75
U.S. Department of Commerce, *U.S. Trade Status with Socialist Countries*, February 19, 1976.

metal, phosphate fertilizer, and lumber; and over 60 percent of the cotton, coal, manganese ore, and wheat imported by the Eastern Europeans.[2]

The Soviet Union, in turn, provides the primary market for a wide range of machinery and equipment exports from the Eastern European nations. In recent years, these nations have increased their imports of machinery and equipment from the USSR and have invested in cooperative development of Soviet raw materials, in order to achieve a better balance in the composition of trade and to ensure the continuity of supply of industrial raw materials to them.[3]

In the first decade following World War II, the Soviet Union and the Eastern European nations minimized the role of foreign trade, each striving for self-sufficiency. Imports were needed for the supply of basic producers' goods to establish a complete industrial base and to alleviate bottlenecks in the domestic supply of raw materials. Exports served only to generate hard currency to finance imports for the industrialization drives.[4] Faced with rising capital/output ratios and increased consumer pressure, however, the Soviet Union, under Khrushchev, began in the early 1960s to deal with slowing rates of growth by taking a technological approach to modernizing industry and by relying increasingly on incentive mechanisms. This new intensive, rather than extensive, approach to economic growth was also adopted by the Eastern Europeans. Trade with the West, then, was encouraged to provide technological and consumer requirements for modernization and an improved standard of living. However, with the exception of Romania, whose turnover with CMEA as a share of the total dropped from 66.9 percent in 1960 to 47.2 percent in 1971, the Eastern Europeans awaited the example and approval of the USSR to open up East-West trade.[5]

A slight surge of Soviet imports from the industrial West began in the late 1960s, bringing the total imports from the developed West up from a 1965 figure of $1.6 billion to $8.0 billion in 14.[6] The major step, the official encouragement of expanded East-West economic relations, came with the Twenty-Fourth Communist Party Congress under Leonid Brezhnev in the spring of 1971. Further stimulus to East-West economic relations was provided by improved political relations with the United States and the Federal Republic of Germany. Commercial agreements were a major part of the accommodations reached between East and West. Aside from massive grain shipments in 1972-73 and again in 1975, the Soviet Union purchased technology and equipment in the West, financed partly by shipments of raw materials and to a significant extent by medium- and long-term credits, both on commercial terms and through government or government-guaranteed credits. The Eastern European nations followed suit, limited to a great extent by their ability to export successfully to hard-currency countries (given limited raw materials export bases) and the willingness of Western countries to extend credit.[7]

Soviet imports from the industrial West grew from $2.5 billion in 1969 to $4.9 billion in 1973, while exports to these countries grew from $2.2 billion to $4.1 billion in the same period. In 1973, 65 percent of Soviet exports to the industrialized West fell into the categories of fuel and crude materials; in the same year, machinery accounted for 32 percent and manufactures 28 percent of Soviet imports from these countries.[8]

Much the same picture can be drawn for the Eastern European nations. For the six countries taken together, imports from the industrial West grew from $2.6 billion in 1965 to $8.7 billion in 1973, while exports to the West grew from $2.3 billion to $7.1 billion in the same period.[9] About one-half of Eastern European exports to the industrial West fell into the categories of agricultural products and crude materials, dropping from 66 percent of the total exports in 1965 to 47 percent in 1971. Imports in the categories of chemicals, industrial semimanufactures, and machinery were 75 percent of total imports from the industrial West in 1971. In the period 1965-72, industrial imports from the West grew at an annual rate of 20 percent for Poland, 18 percent for the GDR, 16 percent for Hungary and Romania, 11 percent for Czechoslovakia, and 8 percent for Bulgaria. In Hungary, the GDR, and Poland the growth of these imports far outpaced the respective growth rates of industrial output of 5, 6, and 9 percent; only in Bulgaria did the latter rate exceed the former.[10]

The People's Republic of China has, by and large, continued to minimize the role of foreign trade in its economy. Growth in trade turnover, however, has exceeded growth of industrial output. While industrial production more than doubled in the period 1965 to 1974, trade turnover rose from $3.7 billion to $13.7 billion in the same period. Trade with the USSR fell from over 10 percent of the PRC's total in 1965 to under 3 percent in 1973, while Eastern Europe's share fluctuated around the 6 percent mark in this period. The industrial West (except the United States) and the developing nations were China's major trade partners throughout the period. Trade with the United States showed up in the statistics only after 1971, but in 1974, 11.8 percent of the PRC's total imports were from the United States. However, these should be seen as selective imports and not necessarily a commitment to increased dependence on trade with the West. Imports from the United States in 1974 were 81.6 percent food and nonfuel raw materials.[11]

Organization and Conduct of Foreign Trade in Nonmarket Economies

The Soviet system of foreign trade, i.e., the state monopoly of foreign trade, served as a model for the system originally instituted in the six nations here considered as Eastern Europe and in the People's Republic of China. In each case, the system remains more or less intact, with each of the NMEs incorporating new features to varying degrees.

In the USSR, all foreign trade is conducted through foreign trade organizations (FTOs), each FTO being responsible for the import and/or export of a specified category of goods. All contracts with foreign enterprises are signed with

FTOs. Operating within the annual plan for foreign trade and for foreign exchange, the FTOs purchase goods at domestic prices from Soviet enterprises and sell them abroad, usually at world market prices if the sale is outside CMEA, or at bilaterally negotiated prices within CMEA. The FTOs operate under the direction of the Ministry of Foreign Trade. The ministry issues permits for imports and exports, approves foreign exchange allocations, and oversees clearing and settlement of transactions. Apart from these day-to-day operations, the Ministry of Foreign Trade negotiates international agreements on trade and payments and maintains trade delegations abroad to expedite Soviet foreign trade operations, issue import permits and country-of-origin certificates, and collect commercial information. In the USSR, a foreign trade bank (Vneshtorgbank) maintains the accounts of the FTOs, extends credit to the FTOs, buys and sells foreign exchange, acts as a correspondent for foreign banks, and handles all operations dealing with foreign currency other than trade, e.g., tourism, overseas remittances, etc.[12]

The Soviet foreign trade organizations are legally autonomous entities. They alone are responsible for their debts, which must be paid out of their corporate assets. The FTOs may own property and are liable to legally binding arbitration in Soviet courts. The FTOs are the sole Soviet organs authorized to engage in foreign transactions in the commodity or service areas defined by their charters. Soviet cooperative institutions may engage in exchanges with similar foreign organs; and several organizations for shipping, film export, tourism, and technical services which do not fall under the jurisdiction of the Ministry of Foreign Trade may deal abroad as well. When these orgnizations engage in international transactions, however, they do so under the guiding hand of the Ministry of Foreign Trade.

The USSR also owns or participates in the mixed management of over forty companies abroad, incorporated and operating under the law of the host country, to provide support services for Soviet foreign trade activities. Amtorg in the United States and Arcos, Ltd., in the United Kingdom act as brokerage firms for Soviet foreign trade transactions. Also in the United Kingdom, Nafta serves as distributor of Soviet oil exports and the Russian Timber Agency as distributor of forestry exports. In Belgium, Scaldia Volga markets Soviet autos, and in Italy, Stanitaliana is a distributor for machine tools. These mixed companies have representatives of appropriate FTOs on their management boards. Shipping services are provided by such mixed companies as Aspo in the United Kingdom and United Oriental Shipping in Japan, while insurance services are handled by still other mixed firms, such as the Black Sea and Baltic Insurance Company of the United Kingdom.[13]

The Soviet Union also maintains an international network of banks: Moscow Narodny Bank in London, Banque Commerciale pour l'Europe du Nord in Paris, Woschod Handelsbank in Zurich, Ost-West Handelsbank in Frankfurt, Donaubank in Vienna, the Russian-Iranian Bank in Teheran, and the East-West United Bank in Luxembourg.[14] These banks have been established to procure credits on more favorable terms and to earn hard-currency profits on normal banking services. While the major activity of the banking network is discounting bills of sale from Western exporters and accepting commercial paper from the Soviet bloc, the banks are also very active in the Eurocurrency market.

Foreign trade in the Soviet Union is planned as part of the five-year and annual plans for the Soviet economy. The annual plan has the force of law and detailed targets are not published. General goals, or control figures, are generated by Gosplan (the State Planning Commission) for imports to meet gaps in domestic production, for the modernization of industry through Western equipment, and in recent years, to support the building of giant, high-priority projects, such as the Kama River Truck plant. The goals for exports are designed to meet obligations to CMEA countries, to secure hard currency for imports, and to support political commitments to developing countries. The control figures for imports and exports go to the planning organs of the Ministry of Foreign Trade and to the ministries which will require import deliveries and ship exports. Recommendations of the ministries and their enterprises as to their requirements and their capabilities to meet the goals are sent back to Gosplan and a second iteration begins. When the foreign trade plan is balanced and reconciled with the annual plan for the economy, a plan for foreign exchange to support these transactions is drawn up and the plans then must be submitted to the Council of Ministers for confirmation. The detailed plan results in directives to the FTO concerning quantities of goods to be exported, inventories to be maintained, transport to be utilized, goods to be imported, the form of payment for imports, and the ministries to which imports are to be delivered. The ministries and material-technical supply organizations arrange for specific export suppliers and import consumers which then conclude formal contracts with the FTOs. Domestic wholesale prices are paid to export suppliers and are charged to import consumers. Since the FTOs must deal in both world prices and intra-CMEA prices, which differ from domestic wholesale prices, and since foreign exchange is allocated to them by the state, resulting deficits are absorbed by the state, thus shielding the domestic enterprises from the direct effects of fluctuations in world markets.[15]

In order to provide stability for planning purposes and to facilitate trade balancing to minimize currency transfers, the Soviet Union (and other CMEA members as well) prefers bilateral trade agreeements. In Soviet trade with other CMEA nations, commodity exchange is bilaterally determined in detail for classes of commodities (i.e., heavy machine tools). In past agreements between the USSR and Western governments, the specifications have often included lists of commodities for which there is a commitment to issue import and export licenses up to stated quotas for given commodities. A commitment to expand credit to the USSR by the Western partner may also be part of the bilateral agreement.[16]

A new form of agreement, the compensation agreement, has arisen in the period since the later 1960s and has resulted in some major transactions between the USSR and Western firms. These agreements are signed directly with the Western enterprises. The compensation or "buy-back" involves repayment for participation in and equipment for the construction in the USSR of productive capacity with future deliveries of the commodity produced. For example, Occidental Petroleum will cooperate in the construction of a complex in the USSR for the production of mineral fertilizer in return for deliveries of part of this production over a period of twenty years. This agreement involves mutual deliveries valued at about $1 billion.[17] Agreements such as this one on a compensatory or buy-back basis are attractive for a centrally planned economy: there is no commitment of hard currency and no involvement of existing productive capacity in production for export, so that this is not a diversion of capacity from domestic purposes in order to finance imports, but rather an investment by the foreign firm in Soviet development.

While the Soviet model has served to present the basic features of the organization of foreign trade by the NMEs, the Eastern European states considered here have relaxed, to some degree, the strict control of foreign trade by foreign trade organizations. Only in the case of Hungary has there been a significant departure from the Soviet model. In Hungary, after price, exchange rate, and tax reforms are instituted, profits are to be the prime determinant of export and import decisions. The number of enterprises with the right to deal directly with foreign firms (they have the option of using the foreign trade enterprises) was over 100 in 1973. The foreign trade enterprises themselves are assuming the role of agents for producers rather than contracting parties.[18] A number of previously existing foreign trade restrictions have been retained, including controls on foreign exchange, quotas, permits for foreign trade, and deposit requirements for import transactions. The practice of government intervention to prevent serious trade imbalances, to protect domestic industry from competition, and to preserve central goverment priorities has also been retained.[19] Since in Hungary import decisions are made by producing enterprises which pay foreign trade prices (including tariffs) rather than domestic prices for the imports, Hungary does employ an operational tariff system, and lack of most-favored-nation (MFN) status for the country of origin results in duty on imports 15 percent higher, on the average, than the duty on imports receiving MFN treatment.[20]

Hungary is experimenting with several new types of relationships between enterprises and foreign trade organizations in cases where FTOs are used. The commission contract provides, to both the producing enterprise and the foreign trade combine, a percentage of any excess of actual price paid by the foreign purchaser over the price predetermined by the enterprise and foreign trade unit. Thus each has an interest in selling an attractive product at a good price. In one type of joint venture contract the producing and foreign trade enterprises cooperate in selling the product; the profit over and above the preset profit goes to the producer, and the commission goes to the foreign trade combine. In pooling arrangements, both production and sales expenses are shared by both parties and total profit or loss is split.[21] In these arrangements, producing enterprises, unlike those in the Soviet case, have a vested interest in meeting the needs of foreign markets.

Poland, like the other Eastern European nations, differs from the Soviet Union in that foreign trade activities are not restricted to the specialized foreign trade enterprises. Poland supplements the activities of foreign trade combines by allowing cooperatives and certain limited liability companies to sell—but not purchase—abroad.[22] In 1970, the direct control of foreign trade by the Ministry of Foreign Trade was further decreased when twenty-five foreign trade enterprises were reorganized—either placed under the direct control of industrial associations (trusts) or attached to industrial ministries. By 1971, the fifteen foreign trade enterprises still directly under the Foreign Trade Ministry were conducting only one-third of Polish sales to CMEA countries and one-half of sales to the West.[23] The intent of these reorganizations was to bring production and foreign trade closer together. The principle of commodity exclusivity (i.e., each foreign trade enterprise holds a monopoly for a given commodity), however, was retained. The production enterprises, therefore, do not necessarily deal with a foreign trade enterprise in the same jurisdiction, and thus separation of the functions is again introduced.[24] The centrally planned nature of foreign trade in Poland has been somewhat diluted by these reorganizations, but the right to purchase abroad, the much more significant reform that is part of the Hungarian model, is not a part of the Polish scheme.

While wide-ranging economic reforms aimed at a market orientation were envisioned for Czechoslovakia by the pre-1967 liberal regime there, the current regime rigorously ensured that central direction of the economy was reasserted. Some decentralization in foreign trade activities, however, was retained. Enterprises whose production is most important to foreign trade are permitted to engage in foreign trade activity (by 1972, the number so authorized had risen to 50). These transactions are handled by joint stock companies consisting of foreign trade associations, industrial associations, and banks. Central authorities do exercise significant control of Czech enterprises' foreign trade activities. The State Bank is charged with increasing the efficiency of foreign trade and has the right to intervene in foreign trade transactions in the national interest.[25]

Romania has moved to integrate foreign trade activity into the framework of domestic economic decision making.[26] Industrial combines, in cooperation with foreign trade associations, are responsible for foreign sales of subordinate enterprises, and upon receiving a permit from the Ministry of Foreign Trade can conclude agreements directly with foreign firms. They can also maintain sales and distribution facilities and conduct market research abroad.[27] The foreign currency receipts earned by enterprises in foreign trade must be remitted to the Foreign Trade Bank, but over-plan surpluses may be retained and used freely. Enterprises are responsible for the fulfillment of foreign trade plans independent of overall plan fulfillment.[28] Another new approach to foreign economic relations in Romania is the institution of joint ventures in which foreigners may own up to 49 percent of the equity.[29]

In East Germany, three types of organizations are authorized to engage in foreign transactions—large enterprises heavily involved in export production, sales enterprises that are subordinate to industrial associations, and foreign trade enterprises directly under the Foreign Trade Ministry. These latter enterprises, in the main, do not purchase goods for sale abroad, but rather deal on a commission basis.[30] Decentralization has not been extended to the East German economic system as a whole, although some reform with respect to managerial incentive systems aimed at stimulating technological innovation has been instituted. East Germany is unique among the CMEA nations in that its goods receive, in effect, essentially the same treatment from the European Community (EC) as do exports of EC members. This is true because, as a result of complex political issues at the time the relevant treaties were negotiated, the Federal Republic of Germany treats transactions with East Germany as internal trade. East German goods can then be reexported to the rest of the EC.[31]

Bulgaria, which has instituted and dismantled a confusing array of economic reforms in the 1960s and 1970s, permitted industrial trusts to engage directly in foreign transactions on an experimental basis after 1965, but withdrew this right in 1968.[32] The current trend is toward recentralization of economic activity in economic complexes (i.e., vertical trusts).[33] A few major enterprises are specifically permitted to engage directly in foreign transactions. In addition, the foreign trade enterprises do carry out transactions on a commission basis for some branches of industry to effect coordination of production and trade efforts. On the whole, however, Bulgaria retains the Soviet organizational model, with a strong Ministry of Foreign Trade coordinating centralized import and export activities.[34]

The foreign trade of the People's Republic of China, much like that of the Soviet Union, is conducted solely by foreign trade corporations (eight in number, as opposed to the Soviet Union's forty-plus). The foreign trade corporations (FTCs) operate a foreign trade plan administered by the Ministry of Foreign Trade. China's foreign trade is cloaked in secrecy. No trade figures are published. The charters establishing the FTCs have never been published, leaving their legal status unclear—the FTCs have no assets abroad and there are no civil courts in the PRC. Although the PRC does not maintain wholly or partly owned companies abroad to handle the necessities of foreign trade, the FTCs do, at times, act through firms in Macao and Hong Kong which serve as agents.[35]

Nontariff Barriers to Western Exports to the Nonmarket Economies

It can be seen from the consideration of the trading systems of NMEs that a number of concepts relevant to nontariff barriers presented by the economic systems of the nonmarket countries can be developed. The foreign trade plan, for example, which has the force of law, can be viewed as the discriminatory application of import quotas. However, quality and technical standards, which are a major element in the consideration of nontariff barriers between Western trade partners, have not been a problem in securing markets for Western goods in the NMEs. Other features of the nonmarket economies which do act as nontariff barriers are peculiar to the NMEs: the lack of commercial information, the separation of the Western businessman from his ultimate customers, poor business facilities, lengthy negotiations, and complex financing arrangements.

The lack of standard commercial information and the peculiar domestic pricing systems of the NMEs prevent the Western businessman from making his accustomed business calculations and from adequately assessing business opportunities in these economies.

The separation of the businessman from his ultimate customers, the producing enterprise and the consumer, by the requirement to negotiate solely with foreign trade organizations prevents the businessman from assessing opportunities and interesting potential customers in his products. This is compounded by the limited personal mobility of the foreign traveller in the NME nations and by the limited travel allowed to citizens of NME countries. These conditions also inhibit the responsiveness to consumers and customer services which play a major role in Western marketing strategy in a wide variety of product areas. This separation of the enterprise from the Western exporter by the FTO applies to a somewhat lesser extent in several of the East European countries than in the Soviet Union and the PRC, as was indicated earlier. Even in the case of the USSR, there are some preliminary indications that, in a selected number of situations, the consuming enterprise will be included in a consultative role in import negotiations in the future.

These problems are further exacerbated by the difficulty of establishing representative offices in these countries. Poland, Czechoslovakia, Bulgaria, and the GDR have established state agencies in their capitals to represent foreign firms, but often their services prove insufficient. In recent years only Poland and Romania have officially encouraged the opening of representative offices in their countries by foreign firms, although such offices are permitted by law in most nations. In the Soviet Union, the accreditation required may be difficult to obtain and hinges on the size of contracts under way with Soviet organizations. Even when authorization can be obtained, office facilities and housing are expensive and difficult to secure.[36]

Although the foreign trade plan can be and often is altered during its implementation, once it has been confirmed, it may represent a significant barrier to the negotiation of commercial agreements not specifically provided for. The planned nature of foreign trade also imposes difficulties in negotiating deals to be executed over a multiyear period, given the uncertainty of NME foreign exchange availability in subsequent plan periods. The tailoring of foreign trade plans to commitments to commodity exchanges called for by existing bilateral trade agreements causes discriminatory application of import quotas—one of the traditional concepts of nontariff barriers.

Large U.S. firms that have made the decision not to try to export to NMEs have cited, besides the barriers delineated above, the lengthy negotiation processes and complicated financing terms they feel are endemic to this trade.[37] The negotiation process for concluding a transaction can prove to be a costly venture, both in terms of the time of key personnel involved and of expenses for travel, lodging, business facilities, etc. The foreign trade negotiator of the NME enjoys the ability to deal at the preliminary stage with a number of Western firms. While in some sense the NME receives some of the benefits of a monopsonist, the Western firm is not obliged to sell to him at unprofitable terms—that is, the firm may choose to accept or reject the terms proferred. Because it and other firms are negotiating with a state trader and not submitting sealed bids or selling to a market, however, its profit margin may be trimmed. In addition, if the Western firm is not selling a product of high enough priority to command hard currency in payment, alternate financing arrangements may be necessary. The Western trading partner may become involved in barter, buy-back, or switch transactions (the latter involves brokers' fees for arranging to market goods). While Western European governments provide credits to finance expanded exports to NMEs, U.S. firms are at a disadvantage due to the de facto prohibition imposed in 1974 on Eximbank credits to the USSR and other non-MFN countries.

In a pattern set by Western European countries in expanding trade with NMEs in the 1960s, the United States has established intergovernmental joint commissions to resolve issues presenting barriers to the normalization of economic relations: the U.S.-USSR Joint Commercial Commission (1972), the American-Polish Trade Commission (1972), and the American-Romanian Economic Commission (1973).[38] The secretary of the treasury is the U.S. co-chairman of the U.S.-USSR commission, and the secretary of commerce is the U.S. co-chairman of the other two. The U.S. Secretariat for the commissions is in the Department of Commerce's Bureau of East-West Trade. These commissions are an institutional response to the unique problems of trading with NMEs, in recognition of the fact that the role of the government in the day-to-day conduct of trade and the scope of government decision making in the trade of NMEs is much broader than in the West. The commissions monitor current developments not provided for by existing agreements, define problems, and attempt to facilitate their resolution. Working groups of the commissions address specific issues in the areas of business facilitation, financing, trade promotion, legislation, and licensing. Very specific results have come from the formulation of texts for agreements on these issues (such as on arbitration, with the USSR, or on airworthiness, with Romania) through the work of the joint commissions, as well as exchanges of information on organizational, legal, and commercial aspects of doing business.[39]

In the private sector, joint councils have been formed, in cooperation with the U.S. Chamber of Commerce, with Bulgaria, Czechoslovakia, Hungary, Romania, and Poland.[40] The U.S.-USSR Trade and Economic Council, with participation by both the U.S. private sector and Soviet organizations, has offices in both Moscow and New York and has been quite active in facilitating commercial contacts and providing a forum for discussion of commercial issues in U.S.-USSR economic relations. The goals of the U.S-USSR Trade and Economic Council are to create a favorable business environment for U.S.-USSR trade, to conduct research on trade opportunities and issues, and also to assist in the conduct of commercial and intergovernmental discussion on trade agreements. The National Council for United States-China Trade, formed by U.S. businessmen, serves as a clearinghouse for commercial information and arranges for trade exhibits and trade delegations in the United States and the PRC.[41]

Trade Barriers Faced by the Nonmarket Economies

The NMEs in their turn face a wide variety of barriers to trade with the United States, both tariff and nontariff. For most of the NMEs, tariff barriers result from lack of MFN status with the United States. The NMEs are also subject to special restrictions that deny them access to the Generalized

System of Preferences in the United States. Quantitative restrictions are applied to U.S. imports from the NMEs as well, in some cases in a discriminatory manner. Finally, NMEs are vulnerable to U.S. measures to counteract market disruption that are specific to trade with them and may be applied in a more arbitrary manner than in market-country trade.

Of the NMEs considered here, only Poland and Romania have been granted MFN status by the United States. Thus, U.S. imports from the NMEs other than Poland and Romania are subject to the Smoot-Hawley Tariff of 1930. One estimate of the total value of unrealized exports to the United States by the USSR and five Eastern European countries in 1971 (only Poland then had MFN status) was between $119 and $292 million (actual U.S. imports from this group were $115 million). Approximately 21 percent of this loss occurred in iron and steel products, 11 percent in clothing, 3 percent in meat, 5 percent in miscellaneous manufactured products, 2 percent in fish, and 58 percent in other product groups.[42] Poland has enjoyed MFN status in the United States since 1960 and Romania since August 1975. Polish experience showed that MFN status did help exports to the United States, although other restrictions operative after 1960 reduced U.S. import response to MFN status for Poland. A Polish study showed that between 1963 and 1967, 59 percent of the $55 million increase in exports to the United States was earned in goods most affected by reduced duties.[43]

The Trade Act of 1974 makes the extension of MFN status to non-MFN countries conditional on a determination by the president that the right of citizens to emigrate from the country requesting MFN without paying more than a nominal fee is not abridged. These provisions may be waived for eighteen months after the adoption of the act and extended for one-year periods if the president finds that this will promote the intention of the provisions. Extension of MFN status is predicated on the existence of a bilateral trade agreement, henceforth subject to approval by concurrent resolutions of both houses of Congress; any bilateral agreement negotiated with Czechoslovakia must include a renegotiation of the settlement on debts owed U.S. nationals.[44]

Most NMEs have been granted MFN status by almost all of the Western European countries. Czechoslovakia, Poland, Romania, and Hungary receive MFN status by reason of GATT membership; the others have obtained MFN status via bilateral trade agreements.[45] While the scope of the limitations varies among countries, Western Europe has in general relied on more wide-ranging quantitative restrictions than those the United States applies on imports from the NMEs. Significant relaxation of Western European quantitative restrictions on imports from NMEs has occurred in the last decade, however, through decisions of the Western trading partner and the bilateral and multilateral (via GATT protocol) agreements. The importance of liberalization of the restrictions to the NME is the degree to which the decision applies to commodities that are a significant part of the exports of that nonmarket economy.[46] A study of West German liberalization found that the increase in the share of the market for affected commodities was 1.5 times that of goods still under the quantitative restrictions. The increases were greatest in the CMEA countries' market shares for chemicals and chemical products, but machinery exports from the CMEA countries also gained.[47] Important barriers still remain, however, and the expanded European Community's Common Agricultural Policy is a significant problem to Eastern Europe.

In addition to limiting the granting of MFN status, the 1974 Trade Act also includes this restriction: access to the Generalized System of Preferences, and duty-free treatment for certain products imported from developing countries, is denied to communist countries unless they already receive MFN treatment, are parties to the GATT and members of the International Monetary Fund and are not controlled by "international Communism."[48]

The U.S. also imposes quantitative restrictions on imports of various commodities. The quotas are either allocated by country or permit all transactions until the quota is filled. These quotas may be general or tariff-rate (duty on above-quota imports is much higher) restrictions. In some cases, the allocation of country quotas discriminates against NMEs, since it is determined by the distribution of U.S. imports in some base period. Most tariff-rate quotas, however, are not on an allocated basis. In addition, the U.S. cooperates in several international commodity exchange arrangements which discriminate in quotas against countries not originally parties to the arrangement. In the case of cotton textiles, import quotas are determined by bilateral trade agreements (with various exporters, including Romania) which must meet standards extablished by the GATT International Cotton Textile Trade Arrangement.[49]

NMEs are particularly vulnerable to charges of dumping and market disruption. The Trade Act of 1974 provides for a market disruption test which can be more easily substantiated than that prescribed by the general escape clause provisions which are applied to market countries. Moreover, the president may extend immediate relief, in the form of special duties, until the International Trade Commission can investigate the charges of market disruption.[50] Since in the NMEs domestic prices and production costs are not readily related to export prices or world market prices, an investigation on that basis to certify dumping is not conclusive, and thus a measure of damage to domestic industry is the criterion. Because U.S. experience with NME producers has been limited, the necessity for socialist producers seeking to enter the U.S. market to come in below market price often exists, and the threat of dumping charges is serious. The case of the Polish golf cars is one example in which dumping duties were applied under the provisions of the Trade Act of 1974.

> On November 19, the Department of the Treasury published in the Federal Register notice of a formal finding of dumping of Polish electric golf cars in the U.S. market. This followed the Treasury Department's determination of June 16, 1975, that Polish golf cars were being, or were likely to be sold at less than fair value and the September 16, 1975, determination of the U.S. International Trade Commission that such imports of electric golf cars from Poland were injuring a

> U.S. industry. Special dumping duties are to be assessed on Polish golf cars imported at less than fair value after March 14, 1975, when Customs' appraisement was first withheld. The assessment is to be applied on case-by-case basis, and imports at fair value are not subject to dumping duties.[51]

On the other hand, in an earlier decision dumping charges concerning Romanian work shoes were found to be unsubstantiated.

While barriers that are specifically a result of legislation to regulate trade have been the major concern of the NMEs, other barriers to expanded exports to the U.S. exist, both legislated and not legislated. For example, manufacturing, technical, and quality standards incompatible with those of the Eastern and Western Europeans exist in the United States, and, in the area of food products, requirements for Food and Drug Administration certification are often difficult to meet.[52]

Summary and Conclusions

Examination of the trade patterns of the NMEs reveals that the USSR and Eastern Europe are their own mutual major trade partners with the exception of Romania. Soviet-East European trade is, in the main, an exchange of Soviet raw materials and fuel for Eastern European machinery and manufactures. East European and USSR foreign trade with the industrial West is growing rapidly, consisting, to a significant extent, of the exchange of Eastern raw materials, agricultural products, and semimanufactures for machinery and consumer goods from the West. The People's Republic of China has, for the last decade, directed 90 percent and more of its trade to the industrial West and the developing countries.

The Soviet model of organization and conduct of foreign trade has served well in describing the foreign trade system of other NMEs in Eastern Europe and the PRC, although a trend to decentralization is evident in many of these countries. A prime example is Hungary, which permits a large number of selected producing enterprises to engage in foreign trade and is reforming pricing, tax, and exchange rate policies in order to permit profits to serve as the chief indicator for foreign trade decisions. In contrast to the USSR, a number of the Eastern European NMEs besides Hungary allow certain producing enterprises to arrange for foreign *sales* only, under Ministry of Foreign Trade supervision. Bilateral trade agreements play a large role in the conduct of the foreign trade of NMEs, and, in the case of intra-CMEA trade, are of a detailed nature and supplement formal plan coordination between NME trading partners.

The foreign trade systems, economic mechanisms, and scarcity of customary commercial information in the NMEs present significant obstacles to market economy exporters. These systemic characteristics serve the purpose of insulating the domestic economy from the fluctuations of the world market and preserve priorities of central authorities throughout the NME. These features, therefore, are not negotiable in the sense of total removal of the nontariff barriers, but modifications in order to limit their impediment to Western exports may serve as some measure of quid pro quo for modifications in what the NMEs see as the major impediments to their entry into the market-oriented economies.

Looking to the future, no uniform trend in the organization and conduct of foreign trade can be seen across all the NMEs. While Hungary has gone the farthest in decentralization of decision-making and reliance on economic indicators of efficiency in directing import and export transactions by enterprises, no clear-cut advantages over the more centralized systems in gaining export markets and efficiently satisfying excess demand at home have been demonstrated to the other NMEs. The USSR, Bulgaria, and East Germany have given no indication that they would consider abandoning strictly centralized decision making in foreign trade, or in the domestic economy, for that matter. Although all the NMEs except the USSR authorize some enterprises to engage in foreign transactions, the authorizations are, for the most part, reserved to selected large enterprises, easily monitored, and for the purpose of sales only. These sorts of controls are necessitated by strict central planning in the domestic economy, inconvertible currencies, and short supplies of hard currency. Even in Hungary, the right of intervention is maintained by the central authorities to prevent imbalances from developing. It is not be be anticipated, then, that the major role of central decision makers in foreign trade will be abandoned by the NMEs in the near future.

We have seen, however, that the organization and conduct of foreign trade does vary among the NMEs (see table II-4). The USSR and Bulgaria are highly centralized and bureaucratized with respect to foreign trade. Romania, Poland, East Germany, and Czechoslovakia have introduced some degree of decentralization, mainly in foreign sales. Only Hungary has made significant departures from the Soviet model with respect to both import and export decision making. Thus, the NMEs should be treated individually in U.S. trade policy. The attribute they all share is significant government direction of foreign trade activity, which necessitates special treatment by the United States to ensure mutual benefit in trade relations. With an individualized approach, U.S. policy makers can better achieve mutually beneficial trade with each NME. While central direction will not be bargained away by the NMEs, the prospect of expanded trade with the United States can be employed to induce the NME to work with U.S. policymakers to facilitate mutual benefit. Such an approach, on a limited scale, is embodied in the work of the joint commercial commissions, which should provide not only a useful forum for discussion, but also a tool for the resolution of outstanding bilateral issues to facilitate expanded trade on a more stable basis.

Table II-4
NME DEPARTURES FROM THE SOVIET MODEL OF FOREIGN TRADE

Practice	USSR	Poland	East Germany	Czecho-slovakia	Hungary	Romania	Bulgaria	PRC
Foreign trade reserved to specialized foreign trade enterprises.	X							X
Foreign trade enterprises operate on a commission or joint basis with producing enterprises.			X	X	X			
Selected producing enterprises may engage in direct foreign sales.		X	X	X		X	X	
Producing enterprises may engage in export and import transactions, subject to intervention by central authorities.				X				
Foreigners may participate in joint ventures on an equity basis.					X	X		

3

The Role of Bilateral Agreements In East-West Trade

Karen C. Taylor

By definition the function of a bilateral agreement is to mutually resolve problems that arise between two countries. A bilateral agreement can address specific issues in isolation, such as taxation, fisheries, grains, or scientific and technical cooperation. While most such specific bilateral agreements are not concerned with general trade issues, many of these specific issues affect trade patterns, and some specific bilateral agreements do serve to facilitate trade in general.

A bilateral agreement can also attempt to cover the full range of trade and economic relations between two countries. This general type of bilateral trade agreement is the main focus of this inquiry. General bilateral agreements can address traditional trade issues such as most-favored-nation treatment, or they can address commercial policy issues such as business facilitation, or they can include some aspects of both trade and commercial policy. The legal force can range from a mere expression of intent to penalties for noncompliance. Although usually concerned with trade and economic policy, the scope of the general bilateral agreement has almost unlimited flexibility and can include any topic of interest to the two parties.

Two distinct forms of general bilateral commercial agreements have been employed in East-West trade negotiations. The first type, the general trade bilateral, deals with reciprocal trade obligations and usually contains safeguards against disruptive behavior. The second type, the general economic and industrial cooperation bilateral, is less binding and seeks to facilitate economic interchange by a variety of methods, but usually through the promotion of industrial cooperation. The latter, despite its less binding nature, has become increasingly important. There are two reasons for this development. The first is the increasing importance of industrial cooperation itself vis-à-vis traditional forms of trade. The second reason is the difficulty many Western nations have had recently in negotiating general trade bilaterals (the United States because of the 1974 Trade Act, and the European Community because of the shift of trade negotiating responsibility from the individual nations to the Commission of the European Community).

In the East-West context, general bilateral agreements tend to have a high political content and have to provide mechanisms for achieving the so-called normalization of commercial relations between nations with very different economic systems. Table III-1 presents a summary of the specific and general bilateral agreements concluded between the United States and the European nonmarket economy countries in the 1960s and 1970s. It provides a survey of the variey of forms a specific bilateral can take, and it strikingly illustrates the increased diplomatic activity with these states between 1960 and 1975.[1]

Despite the increased level of activity in negotiating specific bilateral agreements, only two general trade bilaterals have been negotiated by the United States with socialist countries to date—that with Romania which went into effect as of August 1975, and the general bilateral with the USSR, negotiated in 1972 but which the Soviets did not put into force following the passage of the Trade Act of 1974. A revision of that legislation, or some workable compromise with respect to emigration and credits, would be necessary to fully implement the U.S.-USSR Trade Agreement of 1972.

In contrast, there is no necessity to negotiate a general bilateral with Poland, for several reasons, the prime one being that in 1960 Poland's most-favored-nation (MFN) status was restored by the United States. The United States subsequently agreed to apply its GATT obligations with Poland as contained in the Polish protocol of accession to the GATT.[2] Further, U.S.-Polish relations are supervised by a joint commission. And finally, a number of specific bilateral agreements with Poland have supplied most of the necessary components for a full bilateral relationship.

Because of the numerous asymmetries between nonmarket commercial institutions and those of market-oriented countries, the basic trade-off contained in general East-West bilateral agreements has been to provide MFN status and its attendant benefits for the nonmarket economy (NME) and to provide adequate reciprocity for the market economy (such as improved business conditions), as well as to protect against market disruption in the market economy. Secondly, the general bilateral will usually attempt to stimulate trade, for example through credit provisions and provisions for industrial cooperation agreements. Finally, the general bilateral provides for the monitoring of the relationship and a framework for consultations.

This paper will examine the bilateral agreements negotiated by the United States with the USSR and Romania, as well as the relationship with Poland, in order to investigate in detail the various types of agreements that can be negotiated under given political conditions. The approaches of other Western governments will then be discussed to provide a framework for comparison, followed by a discussion of the trade and commercial policy issues most frequently addressed in bilaterals. The principal purpose of this paper is to examine the role of bilateral agreements in East-West trade, with the objective of assessing their effectiveness as instruments for facilitating that trade and ensuring reciprocity.

Bilateral Agreements and Bilateral Relations

The United States and the USSR

Following the initiatives of the 1960s (see table III-1), 197

Table III-1
SUMMARY OF BILATERAL AGREEMENTS CONCLUDED BETWEEN THE U.S. AND EUROPEAN NON-MARKET ECONOMIES
1960-1975

Country	1960-1969	1970-1975
Bulgaria	Claims—63	Consular—75
Czechoslovakia	Aviation—69; N.Y. commercial offices—67; cotton textiles—69; visas—62	Aviation—72, 74, 75; cotton textiles—73; consular—74
German Democratic Republic		Minute on diplomatic relations—74
Hungary	N.Y. commercial offices —69	Aviation—72, 75; claims—73; consular—72; cotton textiles—70, 71
Poland	Agricultural commodities —60, 61, 63, 64; aviation—65; claims—60; social security—68; cotton textiles—67; visas—63	Agriculture (foreign exchange)—2 in 72, 73, 75; aviation—72; consular—73; fisheries—73, 2 in 75; health—74; maritime—73; scientific & technical cooperation—72; social security—71, 75; cotton textiles—70, 74, 75; development of agricultural trade—74; taxation—75
Romania	Claims—60; cultural relations—69; visas—62, 67, 69	Agriculture—75; aviation—74; consular—73; cultural relations—73; cultural & scientific—75; fisheries—73; investment guarantees—73; general relations—73; trade (general bilateral)—75; cotton textiles—70, 75; taxation—75
USSR	Aviation—2 in 66, 68; consular—68; embassy sites—69; telecommunications—63	Agriculture—73; arms limitation—3 in 72, 2 in 73, 75; peaceful uses of atomic energy—73; aviation—73, 75; cultural—73; economic & technical cooperation—74; embassies —72, 74; energy—74; environment —72; fisheries—10 agreements between 73 & 75; grains—72, 75; health—72, 74; housing—74; maritime— 2 in 72, 73, 76; nuclear war—71, 73; oceanographic—73; scientific & technical cooperation —72; space cooperation—72; telecommunications—71, 75; Kama River purchasing—72, 73; US-USSR Chamber of Commerce—73; transportation—73; taxation—75

Sources: *Treaties in Force,* Department of State Publication (8798), January 1, 1975
Department of State Bulletins for 1975 & 1976

marked the significant opening up of U.S.-Soviet trade. In that year, a $125 million grain sale was negotiated. Discussions of commercial relations were begun and U.S.-Soviet relations were rapidly expanded on all fronts: arms limitation, space exploration, nuclear cooperation. The negotiations begun in 1971, which resulted in the Trade Agreement of 1972, marked the first attempt by the United States to negotiate a general trade bilateral with a socialist country. There was a conscious effort to devise a "model pattern" that would provide a sound basis for a continued commercial relationship with the Soviet Union. To quote Peter Peterson, who conducted these negotiations: "What we are after is a comprehensive series of agreements which will plot a 'critical path' through the issues which divide us . . . to create a long term environment in which business can flourish."[3] "We see this as an evolutionary document, a sort of working prototype."[4]

The Trade Agreement of October 18, 1972, was accompanied by a lend-lease settlement (more precisely, the full schedule of lend-lease payments was tied to the granting of MFN status to the Soviets) and by a determination that the Soviet Union was qualified to receive Export-Import Bank credits. The 1972 agreement included what would be conventionally expected from a general trade bilateral: (1) MFN status; (2) general cooperation and an increase in trade (in this case the stated goal was a tripling of trade over a three-year period); (3) provisions for payments in a convertible currency; (4) national security exceptions; and (5) supervision of the agreement by the Joint Commercial Commission, which had been established in May 1972. In addition, the agreement sought new initiatives and provisions for market /nonmarket relations in the following areas:

1. a market disruption procedure significantly easier to apply than GATT obligations;
2. detailed guidelines for the establishment of a U.S. commercial office in Moscow and a Washington trade representation for the USSR; and
3. provisions for the operation of the different legal systems and arbitration as agreed in commercial con-

tracts, including the possibility of third-country arbitration.

It was also stressed at that time that intensive work was ongoing with regard to copyrights and a tax treaty.[5] Special bilaterals dealing in technical detail with maritime relations, grains, and fisheries were concluded later.

How effective would the 1972 agreement have been, had it been put fully into effect? This question is difficult to answer, but it promised to be a major, practical start toward normalizing commercial relations where no government-to-government relationship had previously existed. The 1972 agreement provided for methods to deal directly with some of the difficult problems arising between two differing economic and legal systems, such as industrial cooperation, business facilitation, market disruption, and arbitration. The agreement only indirectly addressed the issues of market and supply access and exchanges of necessary economic information. Nor were the business facilitation provisions as comprehensive as those which were eventually negotiated with Romania.

The Trade Act of 1974

The legislation required on the U.S. side to implement the 1972 U.S.-Soviet Trade Agreement was debated in Congress over a two-year period. The result was the passage of the 1974 Trade Act and the inclusion of Title IV on trade with non-MFN countries. Title IV of the Trade Act responded to the prospect of expanded economic relations with NMEs in three ways: (1) it specified the minimum content of general bilaterals and attempted to ensure economic reciprocity; (2) it placed certain political conditions on the resumption of normal relations; and (3) it revised certain domestic procedures and ensured closer monitoring of East-West trade. Only the first of these responses will be discussed here.

The intent of Congress to participate more actively in trade negotiations via legislation was clear; there was to be no carte blanche in negotiating bilateral trade agreements. To this end, the Congress established a set of parameters for that elusive concept, reciprocity. Under the terms of the Trade Act, the president may negotiate a general bilateral if such a bilateral promotes economic growth and full employment in the United States. However, the act stipulates, "Each such trade agreement shall provide for mutually advantageous economic benefits" (Sec. 105).

More specifically, bilaterals with NMEs are renewable only if—

> (A) a satisfactory balance of concessions in trade and services has been maintained during the life of such agreement, and
> (B) the President determines that actual or foreseeable reductions in U.S. tariff and nontariff barriers to trade resulting from multilateral negotiations are reciprocated by the other party to the bilateral agreement (Sec. 405).

MFN status can only be granted under the terms of a general bilateral agreement and not via a multilateral institution. Despite this fact, trade concessions (both tariff and nontariff) negotiated multilaterally must be reciprocated by the NME.

Other specific requirements which a bilateral with an NME must fulfill under the terms of the Trade Act are:

1. It must be accompanied by a settlement on any outstanding lend-lease obligations and MFN treatment is applicable only if such lend-lease payments are not in arrears.
2. It must have a safeguard section which provides for prompt consultation and the imposition of import restraints to combat market disruption.
3. The other party must be a member of the Paris Convention for the Protection of Industrial Property and the Universal Copyright Convention (or grant U.S. nationals equivalent rights and protection).
4. The bilateral must provide procedures for settlement of commercial disputes.
5. It must provide for trade promotion, including tourism, governmental commercial offices, and trade fairs,

and "for facilitation of entry, establishment, and travel of commercial representatives."

6. It must provide for consultations reviewing the relationship between the two countries.

Finally, the bilateral can be suspended or terminated at any time for national security reasons, and MFN treatment can be withdrawn by the president at any time, subject to congressional approval.

These provisions cover most of the same points concluded in the U.S.-USSR bilateral, but their net effect is to legally mandate the minimum scope of such agreements. Further, the language is much more specific and detailed than the U.S.-USSR agreement. The industrial property and copyright provisions go beyond what was concluded in 1972 and the business facilitation provisions are much more comprehensive than the ones in the U.S.-Soviet agreement. The market disruption provisions differ in the specificity of language used and in the fact that they define what constitutes market disruption in the U.S. market. (The implications of this will be discussed in a later section of this chapter.)

The significance of the U.S.-Soviet bilateral was that it would have provided nondiscriminatory market access for Soviet goods in the United States via MFN treatment and that it would have provided reciprocal access for U.S. businessmen via improved facilities. The commercial offices provided for in the 1972 agreement were established and the U.S.-Soviet Joint Commission remains to supervise the truncated relationship. Nevertheless, the absence of a general trade bilateral, combined with Eximbank credit limitations, has had a dampening effect on the relationship. The volume of orders lost during 1975 to other Western nations has been estimated at around $1.6 billion,[6] although there is no way to quantify such an outcome with confidence.

The United States and Romania

During the 1960s Romania sought to make its foreign policy progressively more independent of the Soviet Union.

Among the steps it took to further this goal was to become increasingly aggressive in the field of foreign trade generally, and to improve its relations with the United States in particular. President Nixon's trip to Romania in 1969 was the first presidential visit to a Warsaw Pact country. As the U.S.-Soviet relationship unfolded, so did the contacts with the Romanians. Unlike the Soviets, however, the Romanians chose to continue negotiations for a general bilateral under the terms of the 1974 Trade Act (despite reported pressure from the Soviets not to set such an "unfortunate" precedent). The U.S.-Romanian bilateral agreement was signed on April 2, 1975, approved by Congress on July 28, and finalized by an exchange of documents on August 3. As mandated by the Trade Act, the term of the bilateral is three years. However, the first presidential request for renewal of the emigration waiver is established by law as June 1976.

Even a cursory glance will show that the Romanian bilateral negotiated under the terms of the Trade Act is an advanced document greatly evolved from the simpler formulas of the U.S.-Soviet bilateral. All provisions of the Trade Act discussed above are incorporated into it. In addition, the bilateral takes into account the GATT obligations of both governments, but it states, as required by the Trade Act, that in the event of conflict the bilateral shall apply. A joint commission oversees the relationship.

The principal differences between the U.S.-Romanian and the U.S.-Soviet bilaterals are in the extensive business facilitation section provided in the former: the inclusion of clauses on industrial property, industrial rights and processes, and copyrights; extended provisions regarding financial transactions; navigation clauses; and an arbitration provision referring to the International Chamber of Commerce rules of arbitration. The Romanian bilateral goes farthest beyond the Trade Act itself in its business facilitation provisions, which require some thirteen paragraphs in Article IV and fourteen paragraphs in Annex II to describe. These provisions include—

making available information on rules and regulations for commercial representations;

treatment no less favorable than that extended to third countries;

permission to deal directly with buyers *and* users;

facilitation of access to marketing information;

recognition of the advertising function and permission for free imports and exports of advertising materials and samples;

good offices of the government in business facilitation and contract compliance;

development of trade-promoting and trade-facilitating services; and

facilitation of tourism and trade fairs.

The business facilitation annex of the bilateral sets out in detail the rights of parties to operate in both countries, including importation of business equipment and promises to facilitate authorizations for office space and communications equipment; broad flexibility in hiring, compensating and terminating employees; multiple entry visas; and foreign travel.

Although on paper this is an impressive set of undertakings, only experience will demonstrate its effectiveness. The strength of the Romanian desire to improve its foreign trade performance and the U.S. ability to effectively maintain the MFN commitment will ultimately set the pace of compliance.

The United States and Poland

Relations have followed a more normal course with Poland since MFN status was restored to the Poles by the United States in 1960. Poland was admitted to GATT in 1967, with the terms of its GATT obligations set out in a special protocol of accession. U.S. trade with Poland in the 1960s exceeded trade with any other socialist country. Also in the sixties, specific bilaterals were concluded between the two countries in the fields of agriculture, aviation, claims, social security, and cotton textiles. Nevertheless, Poland benefited, as did the Soviet Union and Romania, from the U.S. overtures to the socialist countries in the early 1970s.

In 1972 a U.S.-Polish Joint Economic Commission was established and a general undertaking to triple trade in a five-year period was agreed upon. There followed further specific bilaterals including those on fisheries, health, maritime, and scientific and technical cooperation. It can be seen that the spectrum of U.S.-Polish relations was fairly complete, despite the absence of a general bilateral.[7]

What then is missing? Poland is a signatory to the 1967 Industrial Property Agreement, but while it recognizes mechanical reproduction rights for music, it is not a member of the Universal Copyright Convention. Poland is, however, a signatory on the same basis as the United States to the convention on the recognition of foreign arbitral awards of 1958. While lacking the force of an agreement, the second session of the U.S.-Polish Joint Commission recommended that arbitration clauses be included in contracts and suggested the use of either the International Chamber of Commerce or Economic Commission for Europe rules of arbitration. No business facilitation agreements exist, although this is under the purview of the joint commission. Waiver of reciprocal fees for visas extends to performing artists only. National security exemptions are those of the GATT (which are considerably more highly qualified than those of the bilaterals).

The market disruption provisions would have been the same as in the Polish protocol of accession to GATT, except that the Trade Act, in establishing its less rigorous market disruption criteria, extended them to all "Communist" countries, regardless of their MFN or GATT status. However, the discussions which resulted from the U.S.-Polish Joint Commission have served to facilitate cooperation between the two countries with respect to the establishment of technical-commercial representations, the cotton textile and maritime negotiations, U.S. export licensing procedures, pre-arbitral conciliation, standardized contract language, and "doing business" workshops for U.S. firms.

The absence of a general bilateral agreement with Poland has not greatly hampered the development of U.S.-Polish commercial relations. The availability of MFN status and credits, the many special agreements between the two countries, and the efforts of the joint commission have permitted commercial relations to be conducted on a relatively "normal" basis—normal that is, for East-West trade. One illustration of this is in the area of industrial cooperation projects.

The U.S.-Polish industrial cooperation projects have taken a variety of forms, including a deal with International Harvester for light- to medium-power multipurpose tractors and parts, with the right of exclusive distribution in socialist countries and the right to export elsewhere via the IH sales network; a ten-year agreement with Clark Equipment for the production of heavy axles, with world marketing via Clark International Marketing; a deal with the German branch office of Koehring to build hydraulic excavators; an arrangement with U.S. Steel to produce transformer plates; and a deal with Singer for the simple assembly of sewing machines in Poland, to lead eventually to the installation of the complete production process there.[8]

Western European Agreements

While the preceding sections have roughly outlined the history and shape of recent U.S. commercial agreements with Eastern European countries, the approaches to East-West trade and the bilateral agreements of the Western European nations have been different, in terms of both history and content. In this respect, it is necessary to understand the positions of individual Western European nations as well as the status of the European Community's relations with the Council for Mutual Economic Assistance (CMEA) and with the respective nonmarket economies.

Long-term agreements between Western European and Eastern European nations have been both pro forma and commonplace. During the 1970s, some ninety-eight East-West, long-term, bilateral trade agreements were concluded between European nations, out of a total possible number of 133 different East-West combinations. In addition, in 1975 some 102 long-term intergovernmental industrial cooperation agreements were on the books.[9]

While the European Community (EC) Council of Ministers agreed in 1969 to permit, as an exception to its common trade policy, individual member countries to conclude bilateral trade agreements with Eastern European countries, this exception was terminated as of December 31, 1972. The individual trade agreements expired as of the end of 1974. All new agreements must be negotiated by the Commission (the executive body) of the EC. In actuality trade has continued on much the same basis as before, despite the fact that the old system of bilaterals has not been replaced by any trade agreements negotiated by the EC Commission. Needless to say, in the absence of new bilateral trade agreements, the many individual economic and industrial cooperation agreements being negotiated by the EC member countries (which are not covered under the common commercial policy but which must be reviewed by the EC Commission) tend to supplant some of the functions of a bilateral trade agreement.

Little progress has been made on negotiating new bilaterals because the relationship between the EC and CMEA has not been defined. While there are differences of opinion among the Eastern Europeans, the prospect of having to deal with the EC as a bloc is not an unmixed blessing. Nor are the Eastern Europeans unambivalent about extending the powers of CMEA further into trade matters. However, the Soviet Union, in a recent about-face, has been quite interested in establishing a working relationship between CMEA and the European Community. The problem here is that the EC and CMEA do not perform parallel functions with respect to their member states. CMEA coordinates economic integration and certain aspects of long-term planning; the EC regulates a common commercial policy and a common tariff system.

Initial exploratory talks between the Commission of the European Community and CMEA, held in April of 1975, arrived at no agreement. Indeed, no movement occurred until February 1976, when the CMEA submitted a proposal for an agreement between CMEA and the EC. Among other items, this proposal contains provisions for direct cooperation on exchanges of economic information and forecasts of production and consumption concerning agreed subjects; MFN treatment to be applied between all countries in question; abolition of discriminatory quantitative restrictions; favorable loans; and bilateral and multilateral consultations and agreements. Although the draft does not establish CMEA as a supranational negotiating authority for its member states, neither does it go the full distance required by the EC that the EC Commission shall be the sole negotiator for its member states' trade policy with respect to the NMEs. As of late 1976, discussions between the EC and CMEA had produced no concrete agreement.

In 1974 the Council of Ministers of the EC approved a "model agreement" which has been circulated to the various East European governments. This model would grant MFN status, with the EC's preferential agreements and free trade agreements remaining intact. The Common External Tariff could be reduced if concessions were matched by the NMEs. Liberalization of some quotas is also provided. The safeguard provisions would be triggered at prices lower than "actual value"—that is, lower than the price which similar products would obtain under fully competitive conditions.[10] No response has as yet been received from the NMEs; it is doubtless contingent on the current EC-CMEA discussions. Despite the fact that the replacement of most of the European bilaterals is at a standstill, Romania has been accepted under the EC's provisions to receive the generalized preferences for developing countries and has agreed to negotiate a bilateral textiles agreement with the EC under the GATT Multifiber Agreement.

Franco-Soviet relations. Stemming from the activist foreign policy of de Gaulle, French-Soviet economic relations date back to the mid-1960s. These years resulted in a panoply of cooperation agreements between the French and the Soviets in the fields of nuclear energy, color television, space, and health. The most significant commercial agreement was the joint accord of June 30, 1966, which established the governing principles of the relationship. During the years

1965-1969, France's trade with the Soviet Union increased by 126 percent. However, even this high growth rate was not enough to surpass the performance of either West Germany or Great Britain as the USSR's traditional Western European trade partners. (See table III-2 for a comparison of Western European trade performance.)

Table III-2
TRADE OF SELECT WESTERN EUROPEAN COUNTRIES WITH THE USSR
(in millions of dollars)

	FRG		France		Italy		U.K.	
	Quan.	%Δ	Quan.	%Δ	Quan.	%Δ	Quan.	%Δ
1965								
Ex.	146.5	—	72.0	—	98.1	—	127.3	—
Im.	210.5	—	146.0	—	181.3	—	333.0	—
1966								
Ex.	135.3	− 8	75.8	+ 5	89.3	− 9	139.2	+ 9
Im.	243.3	+16	171.7	+ 18	189.9	+ 5	331.8	0
1967								
Ex.	198.1	+46	155.2	+105	124.9	+40	174.4	+25
Im.	264.8	+ 9	187.0	+ 9	274.6	+45	338.4	+ 2
1968								
Ex.	273.4	+38	256.4	+ 65	179.5	+44	245.0	+40
Im.	292.3	+10	182.8	− 2	285.9	+ 4	379.4	+12
1969								
Ex.	405.7	+48	264.0	+ 3	287.0	+60	231.3	− 6
Im.	334.2	+14	204.4	+ 12	247.1	−14	473.1	+25
1970								
Ex.	422.4	+ 4	273.1	+ 3	307.9	+ 7	244.8	+ 6
Im.	341.6	+ 2	203.5	0	281.5	+14	528.1	+12
1971								
Ex.	460.7	+ 9	255.5	− 6	292.8	− 5	230.9	− 6
Im.	366.3	+ 7	259.6	+ 28	294.9	+ 5	533.5	+ 1
1972								
Ex.	712.2	+55	336.4	+ 32	268.3	− 8	226.4	− 2
Im.	420.7	+15	291.0	+ 12	324.8	+10	561.6	+ 5
1973								
Ex.	1182.6	+66	576.0	+ 71	351.6	+31	238.3	+ 5
Im.	713.0	+69	432.8	+ 49	441.8	+36	807.7	+44
1974								
Ex.	1856.0	+57	660.2	+ 15	618.0	+76	257.3	+ 8
Im.	1222.7	+71	587.6	+ 36	801.6	+81	928.6	+15

%Δ=percentage change from previous year
Source: OECD, Statistics for Trade, Monthly Bulletins

On December 6, 1974, France and the USSR signed a new five-year agreement on economic cooperation.[11] Since it is not technically a trade agreement, it ostensibly does not negate the EC Commission's sole authority over trade negotiations. Informally, both countries established the goal of tripling their mutual trade over the next five years. In addition to general articles concerning implementing their ten-year cooperation program of 1973, the agreement provided facilitation for large-scale cooperation projects and credits. It also contained two business facilitation clauses which, however, lacked the specificity and rigor of those contained in the U.S.-Romanian agreement. By way of example, one might compare the U.S.-Romanian provisions for assisting in the rental of office space and equipment with their counterpart provisions in the French-Soviet agreement:

> Representations shall be permitted to rent office space for their needs and housing. . . . The Parties, upon request, will use the good offices at their disposal to facilitate and expedite the obtaining and occupying of such office space and housing (Article 5, Annex 2 of the U.S.-Romanian Trade Agreement).

> To develop cooperation provided for by the present Agreement, each of the Sides undertakes to give appropriate assistance to organizations, enterprises and firms of the other country and their employees in purchasing or renting appropriate office premises (Article 6 of The French-Soviet Five-Year Agreement on Economic Cooperation).

The main cooperating bodies between the two countries are the so-called Grande Commission at the ministerial level and the Petite Commission at the administrative level. The Petite Commission is charged with the execution of the accords. Further, below these two groups are some thirteen industrial sector subgroups and three horizontal groups, one each on economic information, licensing, and standards. While the Grande Commission and the Petite Commission are roughly comparable to the two U.S. Joint Commissions and their working groups, respectively, no U.S. structure exists which is comparable to the sectoral and horizontal groups, although these have been proposed by the Romanians.

The Federal Republic of Germany and East-West relations. Although the Federal Republic of Germany's (FRG's) economic strength and central location have made it the socialist countries' most important Western European trading partner, the political difficulties stemming from World War II and the general situation deriving from the divided Germanies and Berlin have made the FRG trade negotiations extremely complex.[12].

The German-Soviet bilateral of 1972 can be viewed as roughly equivalent to other German East-West agreements. The respective parties, recognizing the mutually advantageous nature of their bilateral trade, agreed to (1) promote a high volume of trade; (2) further trade liberalization by the reduction of barriers; (3) liberalize existing quotas on imports; (4) conduct trade at world market prices; (5) facilitate a full range of industrial cooperation ventures; (6) facilitate credits; (7) make payments in Deutsche Marks or a fully convertible currency; (8) establish a joint commission and an agreement to consult if respective EC or CMEA commitments raise mutual problems; and (9) accept the standard Berlin and four-power consultation clause. The Germans, like the French, have entered into ten-year economic, industrial, and technical cooperation agreements with the Soviet Union, Romania, Hungary, Bulgaria, and Poland.

In the case of the FRG, however, it is not the provisions of their standardized bilaterals which are most interesting, but the way in which political issues have become linked with economic issues. An example is the recent FRG-Polish credit agreement. The Poles had run a persistent and sizeable trade deficit with the West Germans, and were in the position of approaching the limits of private commercial credits open to them. Added to this were the claims for World War II indemnities against the Germans and social security claims. The Germans, for their part, were dissatisfied with the pace and number of ethnic Germans being permitted to leave Poland. Negotiations between the FRG and Poland on these entangled problems resulted in an agreement, signed on October 9, 1975, involving payment of social security claims in the amount of 1.3 billion DM, and a low-interest, long-term credit of 1 billion DM. An accompanying protocol commits Poland to enable the emigration of from 120,000 to 125,000 Germans over a four-year period. While the parallelism with the emigration provisions of the U.S. Trade Act is striking, the differences are perhaps more important. Despite the fact that the historical and ethnic ties were more compelling and direct, in the German case a particularly sensitive problem was handled as a strictly limited bilateral instrument and was not permitted to spill over into relations with other countries nor to hinder East-West trade relations generally.

Finnish East-West relations. The case of Finland is a special one. Finland is heavily dependent upon foreign trade, and the export sector is particularly important to the health of the Finnish economy. The Finns have close economic links with both the Soviet Union and Great Britain, as well as with the CMEA countries and Western Europe. As a result, Finland's economic situation and trade flows demand a Janus posture, as Finland faces both East and West. Finland is a member of GATT and the OECD and is associated with the European Free Trade Association. Since 1960 it has had a special customs agreement with the Soviet Union. In addition, it recently concluded a cooperation agreement with CMEA and agreements for free trade areas with Bulgaria, Hungary, the GDR, and Czechoslovakia. Finland is currently negotiating similar agreements with Romania and Poland.

The Finnish bilaterals establishing free trade areas take on the special form of a free trade agreement and are, of course, more trade-policy-oriented than the standard Western European economic cooperation agreements or even the U.S. bilateral with the Soviets. The Finnish agreements include schedules for customs duty reductions; elimination of customs-duty-like charges; a freeze on quantitative restrictions and their eventual elimination; a rather detailed but broad safeguard section;[13] exceptions for balance-of-payments action; standard health, public safety, and national security exceptions; and the establishment of joint commissions authorized to implement the agreements. 1985 is the date set for the reduction of tariffs to the zero level.

The Finnish Free Trade Agreements are currently being reviewed by a GATT working party to ascertain whether they conform to the free trade area provisions of Article XXIV. Aside from the legal GATT requirements, however, it is important to ask whether meaningful free trade areas can be established with NMEs where barriers other than tariffs are more significant in limiting mutual trade. The Finns obviously came to the judgment that the political and economic benefits of a free trade agreement with these countries would outweigh the problems caused by the different economic structure of the NMEs. And the Finnish-Czech agreement attempted a unique approach to this problem by including a reciprocity-by-other-means clause, which reads as follows:

> Czechoslovakia shall use the means provided by the Czechoslovak economic system which, in addition to customs duties, have a bearing on the access of Finnish goods to the Czechoslovak market in a manner which will provide for the Finnish exports advantages corresponding to those enjoyed by the Czechoslovak exports on the Finnish market as a result of the liberalization measures taken by Finland under this Agreement (Article 9).

Summary

What can be summarized from the above catalogue of differences? First, for the United States the main issue has been whether or not to grant MFN status to the NME states, although the Europeans have readily granted MFN status while maintaining a quota system. The United States has pushed business facilitation more vigorously, while the Europeans have actively sought increased information about plans and forecasts. The United States has been more concerned with the legal character of its agreements, while the West Europeans have regarded the bilateral as being largely pro forma.

The contrast between the United States and Western Europe is quite clear. For political reasons, the United States has been ambivalent about initiating a long-term trading relationship with the East on a commercial basis. The West Europeans, who hold a no less hard-headed view of the political and economic risks involved in trading with the USSR and Eastern Europe, chose to proceed, established the official channels, and had confidence in their own ability—backed up by their quota system—to meet and overcome whatever problems might occur. The West Europeans actively sought to expand East-West trade, despite the fact that, due to the proximity of NME nations, their economies were more penetrable and thus more vulnerable.

Over the past few years the emphasis in bilateral agreements has increasingly shifted from a concentration on MFN status and quantitative restrictions to industrial cooperation, joint ventures, technology transfer, credits, and marketing. This has been due to two factors. One has been the recent difficulties for both the United States and Western Europe that have hampered the negotiation of standard trade agreements, which tend to focus more on MFN status. But also the shift has been due to the increasing importance of the issues mentioned above to the smooth functioning of East-West trade.

In addition to an appreciation of the anatomy and taxonomy of the bilateral, an understanding of the basic issues is necessary. The agreements which have been described above have, to summarize in rather general terms, addressed themselves either to commercial issues or to trade policy issues, in diverse combinations. Some of the more important commercial issues (business facilitation, industrial cooperation, credit) and trade policy issues (MFN status and quotas, market disruption) are discussed below. Tables III-3 through III-6 set out the policy instruments most directly affecting these issues in the United States and Europe.

Table III-3
COMMERCIAL POLICY ISSUES AND REGULATORY INSTRUMENTS FOR THE U.S. AND SELECT NMEs

	Business Facilitation				Industrial Cooperation	Government Credits	Claims Settlement
	Business Conditions	Industrial Property Rights	Arbitration	Taxation			
U.S.-USSR	Joint Commission[a]; L-T Ag. on Ec., Indus. & Tech. Coop. '74	UCC '52; Union of Paris '67	Joint Commission[a]; individual contracts; CSCE	Treaty ratified Dec. '75	L-T Ag. on Ec., Indus. & Tech. Coop. '74; individual contracts	Eligible for Eximbank loans qualified by Trade Act of 1974	Lend-Lease Agreement of 1972 in suspension
U.S.-Romania	Trade Agreement of 1975	'75 Trade Agreement; Union of Paris '67	'75 Trade Agreement; Joint Commission; individual contracts; CSCE	Treaty ratified Oct. '75	Statement on Ec., Indus. & Tech. Coop. '73; individual contracts	Eligible for Eximbank loans	Treaty of 1960
U.S.-Poland	Joint Commission[a]	Union of Paris '67	Joint Commission[a]; individual contracts; CSCE	Treaty ratified Oct. '75	Joint Commission[a]; individual contracts	Eligible for Eximbank loans	Treaty of 1960

[a] Joint Commissions normally monitor the entire bilateral relationship. They are cited first in a category only when no other instrument effectively addresses the issue.

Table III-4
COMMERCIAL POLICY ISSUES IN SELECT EUROPEAN-NME BILATERAL AGREEMENTS

	Business Facilitation	Industrial Cooperation	Government Credits	Claims Settlement
France-USSR	Economic Cooperation Agreement of 1975	Ten Year Agreement of 1973; Ec. Coop. Agreement of 1975	Economic Cooperation Agreement of 1975	N.A.
Germany-Poland	Mixed Commission	Ten Year Economic Cooperation Agreement of 1974	Special Agreement of 1975	Special Agreement of 1975
Finland-Czechoslovakia	None	Individual Contracts	N.A.	N.A.
EC "model bilateral"[a]	—	—	—	—

N.A. = not applicable
— = not reported to be in draft
[a] Text of draft not available

Table III-5
TRADE POLICY ISSUES AND REGULATORY INSTRUMENTS FOR THE U.S. AND SELECT NMEs

	Trade Expansion	MFN	Safeguards			Quota *et al.*[a]	Export Controls
			Market Disruption	Anti-Dumping	Counter-vailing		
U.S.-USSR	Basic Principles of Relations of 1972 (general)	N.A.[b]	Trade Act of 1974	Trade Act of 1974	Trade Act of 1974	Grains Agreement of 1975	Export Administration Act
U.S.-Romania	Trade Agreement of 1975 (triple '75-'78)	Trade Agreement of 1975; GATT	Trade Agreement of 1975; Trade Act of 1974; GATT	Trade Act of 1974; GATT	Trace Act of 1974; GATT	Cotton Textiles 1970; 1975	Export Administration Act
U.S.-Poland	Joint Commission (triple '73-'77)	GATT	Trade Act of 1974; GATT	Trade Act of 1974; GATT	Trade Act of 1974; GATT	Cotton Textiles '67, '70, '74, '75; Agriculture 1974	Export Administration Act

[a] Quota, voluntary export agreements, orderly marketing or purchasing agreements.
[b] Does not receive MFN.

Table III-6
TRADE POLICY ISSUES IN SELECT EUROPEAN-NME BILATERAL AGREEMENTS

			Safeguards				
	Trade Expansion	MFN	Market Disruption	Anti-Dumping	Counter-vailing	Quota *et. al.*[a]	Export Controls
France-USSR	Informal Agreement to double & attempt to triple '75-'80	YES	EC-Rules for Imports from State Trading Countries	GATT	GATT	(lapsed trade agree-ment—quota still in effect)	COCOM
Germany-Poland	Economic Cooperation Agreement of 1974	YES	EC Rules for Imports from State Trading Countries	GATT	GATT	(lapsed trade agree-ment—quota still in effect)	COCOM
Finland-Czechoslo-vakia[b]	Free Trade Agreement of 1974 (general)	YES	Free Trade Agreement of 1974	GATT	GATT	abolished as of 1975	N.A.
EC "model bilateral"[c]	YES (general)	YES (reciproci-ty to be negotiated)	YES	GATT	GATT	quota reduction	N.A.

[a] Quota, voluntary export agreements, orderly marketing or purchasing agreements.
[b] Also with Bulgaria, GDR and Hungary
[c] Text of draft not available.

Commercial Policy Issues

Business Facilitation

Business facilitation is a paramount issue both for the United States and Western Europe. The emphasis on it has been greater in the United States because of geographic distance and the relative absence of historical trade relations with the NMEs. The Europeans, because of their closer social and cultural ties, have found ways to bypass official channels, while the Americans have attempted to guarantee access for businessmen by using official agreements. However, the Western European countries would like to simplify their own business operations as well and have started to include such provisions in their agreements.

One of the important business facilitation issues is freedom of travel within the socialist country. This requires the issuance of multiple entry visas. The freedom of travel must be safeguarded. Without it, there is no possibility of achieving another critical need of the businessman: the need to deal both with the official purchaser (the foreign trade organization) and the user (the factory). The U.S.-Romanian agreement, for example, was most specific on this point, despite the liberal use of qualifying phrases:

> The Parties affirm that no restrictions shall exist in principle on contacts between representatives of American and Romanian firms, companies and economic organizations. To this end, representatives of firms, companies and economic organizations of either Party shall be permitted within the territory of the other Party to deal directly with buyers and users of their products, in accordance with the procedures and regulations applicable in each country (Article IV, paragraph 6).

It is also significant that in some of these agreements the right to foreign travel by foreign businessmen is also protected.

There are many more specific needs that could be subsumed under the general rubric of the right to do business: (1) timely processing of the application to establish an office; (2) prompt import and export of business equipment without excessive duties; (3) liberal authority with regard to employment practices; (4) access to adequate communication facilities; (5) ability to house and establish the families of businessmen satisfactorily; and (6) facilitation, where possible, of the advertising function.

The Final Act of the Conference on Security and Cooperation in Europe (CSCE) signed at Helsinki in 1975 covers many of these issues, including improved contacts at all levels, but especially between sellers and users of products and services "for the purpose of studying commercial possibilities, concluding contracts, ensuring their implementation and providing after-sales services"; improvement of working conditions for commercial representations; and the provision of information on legislation and regulations relating to representations.

There is also the issue of confidentiality of business communications. This issue is only indirectly treated in the U.S.-Soviet agreement, which permits the respective commercial offices to operate in cipher. However, the confidentiality-of-communications issue is not readily amenable to intergovernmental agreements and requires adjustments in such practices as conducting business from a park bench. However, combining the difficulty of keeping internal communications confidential with the difficulty of obtaining reliable information about plans and purchasing needs compounds the problem and increases the potential for the foreign trade organization (FTO) to play companies and national representations off against each other. This problem is most serious in the Soviet Union where the size of the market, the difficulty of doing business there, and the bargaining power of the FTOs can distinctly disadvantage all but the largest corporations. This means that the large multinational corporations such as General Motors and Western European state enterprises such as the Italian ENI have an advantage over most other Western firms. In the

Eastern European countries these problems are not as grave, but can occasionally be troublesome.

There are two possible methods of strengthening the businessman's hand on these matters. The first is to permit more cooperation among firms selling to NMEs. However, this runs afoul of U.S. antitrust law and philosophy. The second is to encourage the government to take a more active role on behalf of business. This is not an entirely happy solution either, because Americans are traditionally suspicious of business-government links. Currently the only method available to the U.S. government is to reduce the information handicaps in dealing with CMEA state-trading organizations. This involves requesting and distributing economic information, both macroeconomic and at the enterprise level, about the CMEA economies. Information exchanges are included in most bilaterals, as well as in the Helsinki accords, and are within the purview of the work of the joint commissions.

Despite some progress, the improvement of business conditions will continue to be difficult. As this process evolves, however, the expectations of both parties should begin to match up with the reality of doing business, and the reality of doing business will have veered in the direction of satisfying expectations. As long as trade is beneficial to the East and necessary for CMEA countries' economic development, the incentive to improve the climate of business operations will exist.

Industrial Cooperation

The Economic Commission for Europe has defined industrial cooperation as follows:

> Industrial cooperation in an East-West context denotes the economic relationships and activities arising from (a) contracts extending over a number of years between partners belonging to different economic systems which go beyond the straightforward sale or purchase of goods and services to include a set of complementary or

> reciprocally matching operations (in production, in the development and transfer of technology, in marketing, etc.); and from (b) contracts between such partners which have been identified as industrial cooperation by Governments in bilateral or multilateral agreements.[14]

In short, industrial cooperation agreements (ICAs) can take any number of forms—from simple licensing agreements to coproduction and even joint ownership.

ICAs, both the individual contracts for specific projects and the intergovernmental agreements seeking to encourage industrial cooperation, have multiplied in the last decade and have the potential to stimulate economic relations in a much more dynamic way than trade in the traditional sense. This stems from the fact that the greater the barriers to traditional forms of trade, the greater will be the stimulus to the growth and expansion of industrial cooperation. Since the differences between the two economic systems pose substantial barriers to trade, it follows that industrial cooperation has a great attraction in the East-West context.

Some of the more important factors which make ICAs attractive to the NMEs are the long-term nature of the relationship, technology transfer, and the potential for world-wide marketing arrangements. The incentive for the Western nations is the increased ability to do business, the opportunity to limit the instances when it is necessary to deal exclusively with FTOs, and, for the West Europeans, the occasional opportunity to avoid the often clogged and rigid trade channels.

In the German case, for example, items supplied by a joint project can be regarded as transfers not subject to quotas that would otherwise prevail on goods imported in the normal fashion. The United Kingdom has agreed with Hungary, Poland, Czechoslovakia, and Romania that quotas on products from a joint project can be altered upon request. Consideration is made on a case-by-case basis.[15] The Poles hoped to insert a clause in the Polish-German cooperation agreement that goods produced in joint venture projects could enter Germany free of quota *or tariff* restraints. The

Germans reportedly were not unwilling to do this, but decided against such a provision in the face of an EC protest that such an action constituted a violation of the EC common commercial policy and GATT obligations.[16] Many European nations have simpilfied customs procedures with respect to products from joint projects, and broadly interpret the regulations on temporary admission for processing of goods from joint ventures.[17]

The role of the long-term intergovernmental bilateral economic cooperation agreement has been to (1) identify suitable industries and opportunities; (2) encourage the interest of business; (3) facilitate the conduct of business; (4) encourage a stable relationship; (5) place an imprimatur on this form of cooperation; and (6) via the mechanism of the joint commission, investigate problems that might be preventing or impeding the progress of a contract or an industry-to-industry relationship.

There are several problems relating to industrial cooperation which have serious implications for the economic structure of the Western nations. The first of these is the issue of ownership—or, more specifically, effective control of management decisions. Romania and Hungary permit foreign joint ownership, limited to a 49 percent share of the equity participation.[18] Experience with joint ownership ventures has been limited in Romania, and not until late in 1975 did two Hungarian organizations complete an agreement with Corning Glassworks for a joint venture (Corning has 49 percent interest and Hungary a 51 percent interest) for the production of blood-gas analyzers.[19] However, joint ownership is not always the only or even the best method of controlling management decisions. For example, management services themselves can be packaged and leased (there are indications that the Soviets may be thinking along these lines). Productive facilities can be leased and the leases returned to the host government at the end of an agreed period.

The entire area of industrial cooperation modes is quite flexible. It can be expected that these agreements will increase in number and scope (assuming a continued desire to do business on all sides) and will create patterns of international business flows similar to those created by multinational enterprises. In fact, one author suggests that East-West economic cooperation projects could provide valuable lessons to multinational corporations now struggling with national priorities and social goals.

> These [socialist] societies, which claim to give priority to the so-called "social costs" of economic activities, are in many ways a caricature of the growing trend in Western societies toward taking into account the social costs of capitalism. Successful entrepreneurs in East-West commerce will be demonstrating that they can survive and profit in a different economic and social context. In this sense, East-West trade and industrial cooperation may be an excellent training ground for many of those managers who will be responsible for charting new directions for the Western corporation in the years to come.[20]

Another issue with regard to industrial cooperation projects is the means of effecting payment. Payment in convertible currency is the most straightforward, but not always the most prevalent, form of payment. Arrangements to be paid back in product for a manufacturing industry or in raw materials for an extractive industry are common. A major difficulty for the Western economy is the price valuation placed on the goods accepted as payment. When dealing with a centrally planned economy, it becomes difficult to detect whether prices reflect the true economic costs of production and distribution of natural resources, or whether they represent massive dislocations (subsidies) of the socialist economy to achieve a specific goal. Further, the more advantageous the repurchase agreement is for the Western businessman, i.e., the lower the price of the product used for payment, the more potentially disruptive it is to the functioning of the market system, because the more likely it is that significant subsidization has occurred, thus putting competing Western firms at a disadvantage. The NME countries would of course like to see repurchase arrangements officially approved in bilateral agreements with Western governments. However, since the conditions of repurchase can have disruptive domestic economic effects, individual repurchase arrangements should be carefully evaluated as to whether their trade-creating or trade-distorting effects have greater economic significance.

In sum, industrial cooperation is a form of economic activity which differs from the traditional importation and exportation of goods across national boundaries. ICAs involve transnational economic cooperation at the enterprise and company level. Industrial cooperation not only facilitates the exchange of goods, it also enhances the mobility of such factors as technology, managerial skills, and capital.

Insofar as industrial cooperation is conducted by large national and multinational corporations, it is subject to criticism on much the same grounds as direct foreign investment (lack of effective national control, pervasive and unregulated effects on both home and host economies). These arguments are not as relevant in East-West trade for the following reasons. First, the CMEA countries can be expected to regulate the activities undertaken in industrial cooperation agreements to prevent any harmful effects from weakening their own economies. Certainly the Western economies, with their continued emphasis on quotas, safeguards against market disruption, and technology control and export licensing, have taken precautionary measures. And second, where normal trade channels are impeded by structural rigidities such as exchange controls and state trading practices, industrial cooperation can accomplish the economic interchange which would take place if more normal trade practices were in use. Finally, in the absence of a mutual agreement to liberalize trade, industrial cooperation is the only avenue of access to the NMEs which permits sufficient flexibility for rapid and mutually beneficial growth.

Credit

The role of governments in facilitating credits to NMEs is another crucial variable in trade expansion. In fact, most bilateral agreements (either trade or economic cooperation) of the Western countries, with the exception of those of the United States,[21] have a clause recognizing the importance of credits to East-West trade and agreeing to extend credits on favorable terms.

The competition to provide favorable loans has been keen, and the degree of subsidization involved is difficult to determine. Until recently there was little conformity among the Western governments concerning official credit policy (as can be seen from table III-7), and in many cases special terms applied to Eastern European countries. Talks had been going on for some time among OECD countries in an attempt to arrive at a "gentleman's agreement" on the terms of government-financed and government-insured credits. In July 1976 the talks resulted in the adoption by the governments of France, the United Kingdom, the Federal Republic of Germany, Japan, Canada, Italy, Belgium, and the United States of Unilateral Declarations on Export Credit Terms. The unilateral declarations, which cover the period of one year, set out minimum interest rates and maturities for loans to developing countries (with a per capita GNP of less than $1,000), intermediate countries (with a per capita GNP of between $1,000 and $3,000), and highly developed countries (with a per capita GNP of over $3,000). All the Eastern European countries as well as the USSR would fall in the intermediate category, which stipulates interest rates of 7.25 percent for loans of two to five years and the same rate for loans of over five years. The maximum maturity for loans to intermediate countries is eight and one-half years. Exceptions to the guidelines can be made if seven days' advance notice is given and if consultations among the government credit agencies are conducted. Also, the interest and maturity guidelines do not apply to agricultural commodities, aircraft, and nuclear power plants. One result of these arrangements is expected to be improved information about long-term credits. As can be seen, there is still ample room for differing government credit policies. These one-year declarations are, however, a step in the right direction, and should limit the tendency for national governments to carve out special market shares for their respective nations through the instrument of government-supported credit programs. Hopefully, these declarations will also curb the practice of using credit facilitation clauses in bilateral agreements to assist in fostering national credit policies.

Table III-7
OFFICIAL EXPORT CREDIT TERMS

Country	% of Financed Portion [a]	Maturity of Contracts	Interest Rate % P.A.	% of Supported Exports
U.S.	30-85	Up to 5 years	8.5-9.0	15
		Over 5 years	8.6-9.3	
U.K.	85	2 to 5 years	7.5-8.0	40
		5 to 10 years	8.0-9.0	
France	80-85	2 to 5 years	6.3-7.2	25
		6 years and over	7.5	
FRG	85-90	1 to 11 years	6.3-7.2	7
		4 to 10 years	7.8-8.5	
Italy	85	5 years and over	8.0-9.5	4
		(high priority)	7.0-8.0	
Japan	45-90	2 to 12 years	7.6-8.6	45

[a] Including guarantees.
Source: *East-West Markets*, February 9, 1976

Trade Policy Issues

As can be inferred from the analysis so far, the commercial policy concerns of most bilaterals address the market and supply access issue via business facilitation clauses, in coproduction and marketing agreements, and by facilitating and extending credits. Trade policy issues addressed in bilaterals are similarly matters of guaranteeing equitable market and supply access through the application of MFN treatment and the mutual agreement by both countries to increase trade. Traditionally, market access has been the primary concern. However, the assumption that a free and competitive market would generate an increased and dependable supply has been belied by the production restraints, price increases, and supply interruptions witnessed in various commodities in recent years.

One approach to the supply access issue was made by the U.S.-USSR grains agreement. The interesting aspect of this agreement is the concept that part of the responsibility for guaranteed supply access rests with the buyer, who has the responsibility to act in a nondisruptive fashion. In the case of the U.S.-USSR grains agreement, the USSR was given the choice between purchasing U.S. grains within an upper and lower limit, or not being able to purchase in sufficient quantities to meet their needs. This suggests that supply access, like market access, is a two-sided affair, with the responsibility (on the importing nation in the case of market access, and on the supplier in the case of supply access) to provide open access to the respective markets and export commodities. The counterpart obligation in market and supply access issues is the responsibility on the part of the exporter and on the part of the purchaser to behave in a nondisruptive, nonpredatory fashion.

In contrast, traditional trade policy, as found in a trade bilateral, has sought both to guarantee market access through the extension of MFN status and to protect against abuses of free market access by restricting the granting of MFN status, by quotas, and by market disruption clauses.

MFN Status and Quotas

The principle of MFN treatment has a long history. The majority of MFN tariff obligations today are governed by prevailing GATT interpretations, since most major trading nations are GATT members. For example, MFN rates of duty apply to all countries which have been granted MFN status by a GATT member, whether or not the recipient countries are GATT members themselves and whether or not they have participated in tariff-reducing negotiations.[22]

MFN status essentially seeks to guarantee treatment between two trade partners equivalent to that granted to third countries. The U.S.-USSR bilateral, for example, extends MFN status to customs duties and procedures, internal taxation and handling of imported goods, charges on international transfer payments, and import-export rules. Exceptions to this principle include facilitation of frontier traffic, preferences granted in recognition of UNCTAD resolution 21 of 1968, existing multilateral agreements, and safeguard actions and national security.

Western European nations have granted MFN status quite liberally to NMEs because the Western European countries had a quota system which could efficiently prevent undesired products from entering their markets at unacceptable levels. This quota system includes both individual-country quotas and quotas for the EC as a whole. The system has been liberalized to a considerable degree, but continues to cause problems for the NMEs (e.g., Bulgaria, with respect to beef). As might be expected, the individual countries, with a few exceptions such as Italy, have liberalized their quotas to a greater extent than has the EC.

Both the granting of MFN status and the liberalization of import quotas involve the commitment to open up the home market to foreign imports. This is the basic commitment that must be made by the market economy. In the case of the NME, MFN status and external quotas have little relevance because NME tariffs are usually not high in the first place, but, more importantly, because tariffs do not affect the marketability of products within the NMEs. Further, external quotas need not be imposed when an implicit quota system—the central plan—applies. It is not the NMEs' tariff structure, it is their economic structure and the resulting commercial environment, which impedes the flow of Western products into the NME. This is the reason that business facilitation, arbitration, and flexible regulations for joint ventures are sought as partially equivalent commitments to tariff liberalization.

Market Disruption

In the case of a market economy trading with a nonmarket economy there is a perceived need for effective safeguards and market disruption clauses because of the differences between the two economic systems.[23] Apart from outright quotas and other nontariff barriers, two main avenues of protection exist—an escape clause or market disruption system, and antidumping and countervailing regulations.

The standard, i.e., non-communist-country, safeguard provisions of the Trade Act of 1974 require that imports increase in such quantities as to be a "substantial cause of serious injury or threat thereof" before remedial action becomes available. Substantial cause is defined as a cause which is (a) important and (b) "not less than any other cause" (Sec. 201).

The clauses in both the Romanian and Soviet bilaterals provide for consultation and possible safeguard action under conditions which cause, threaten to cause, or significantly contribute to market disruption. The 1974 Trade Act, however, applies less rigorous criteria of injury with regard to "Communist" imports than does the general escape clause and makes no exception for Poland and Romania, which receive MFN treatment and are GATT members. For "Communist" countries, under the 1974 Trade Act, "market disruption" is defined as the condition when imports are increasing rapidly, "either absolutely or relatively, so as to be a significant cause of material injury or threat thereof" (Sec. 406).

There are two significant points to be noted about this definition. The first is the shift from "substantial cause of serious injury" to a "significant cause of material injury." Since "material injury" is not defined for purposes of this section of the 1974 Trade Act, it is open to a wide range of interpretations. Nor does "significant" yield to the same degree of precision as does "substantial." The second point of note is the "absolute or relative" qualifying provision. It is impossible, starting from a base of virtually zero imports in many categories of products, as is the case with many NME products, to avoid a "relatively" rapid increase.

While these provisions may seem overly protective, an effective safeguard system must be workable within the given political context. The GATT safeguards clause is seldom used because its criteria are difficult to meet, because it must be applied on an MFN basis, and because the way is left open for the other party to take countermeasures. As a result, less desirable forms of protection have been used. In the case of NMEs it is particularly necessary to have an effective market disruption provision because the two other protective devices, antidumping and countervailing regulations, require criteria and issues (sales at less than fair market value and government subsidization) which are not relevant to the economic patterns of an NME.

The difficulty of invoking an antidumping duty on a nonmarket country is vividly illustrated by the recent Treasury and International Trade Commission (ITC) determinations on Polish golf cars. Because Poland lacks a rational price structure, not to mention a golf course, a Polish production price had to be "constructed" by the U.S. Treasury for the Polish cars. This was done by using the cost of production in a third country as the determinant of a "fair" market price—in this case, Canada. In the Polish case the U.S. Treasury determined that the dumping margin exceeded 20 percent and that 100 percent of the sales of Polish golf cars in the United States were made at less than fair market value. The fact that this margin was virtually the same as the degree to which Polish cars undersold domestic cars weighed heavily with the ITC commissioners in their decision that a U.S. industry was being injured. The decision was particularly frustrating for the Poles, who, having been told repeatedly that in order to increase their exports they would have to improve their marketing techniques, heeded this advice, sharpened their pencils, and identified a product which they could supply to the U.S. market to earn some much-needed foreign exchange.

It is interesting to ask whether the importation of Polish golf cars would have been deemed to have resulted in market disruption under the provisions of the 1974 Trade Act. While the market disruption provisions of the 1974 Trade Act are obviously subject to a range of interpretations where no precedents have yet been established, it is clear that if the provisions had been in force the question of pricing at "fair" market value would not have clouded the issue to the extent that it did. In the dumping case, cause of injury was established by the coincidence of the pricing differential. Had the case been brought up under the market disruption provisions, the exercise of constructing a price would not have distracted from the conditions of proving "significant cause of material injury." Further, consultations would have been required and adjustment could have been made by the Poles during this time.

No countervailing duty case has yet been brought against an NME. First of all, subsidies, the unfair trade practice which requires the imposition of a countervailing duty, have never been satisfactorily defined with regard to market economies, much less with regard to nonmarket economies. A different set of standards is required in the case of NME subsidization practices, because while subsidization is considered "bad form" in a free market situation, it is one of the main policy instruments of a centrally planned economy. Secondly, contrary to GATT practice, but due to the peculiarities of U.S. legislation, no injury need be proved on dutiable articles. The latitude of a statute that has no satisfactory definition of the transgression and no criteria regarding domestic impact is immense. Such latitude cannot promote the efficient and steady growth of East-West trade because it increases the uncertainty of exporting to the United States. A summary of the different effects of market disruption, antidumping regulations, and countervailing regulations on market and nonmarket trade is charted in figure III-1.

It can be seen from figure III-1 that only a market disruption procedure evaluating the impact of injury in the domestic market affects trade with both market and nonmarket economies in the same fashion. The imposition of antidumping duties on NME imports threatens trade in all products where a pricing differential exists. The result of such an imposition would either be that the NME would

Figure III-1
The Impact of Different Safeguard Measures on Market and Non-Market Trade[(a)]

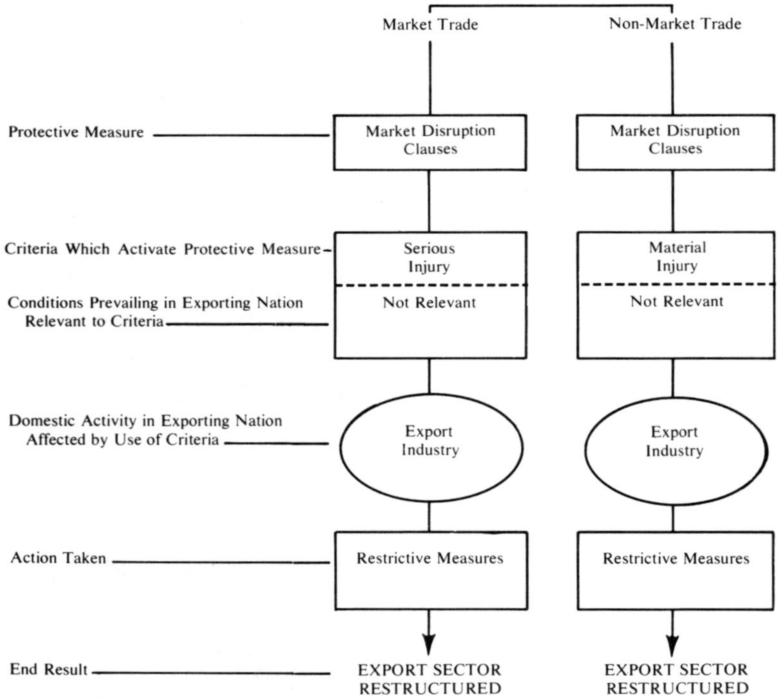

(a) Trade between market economies on the one hand, and trade between market economies and non-market economies on the other hand.

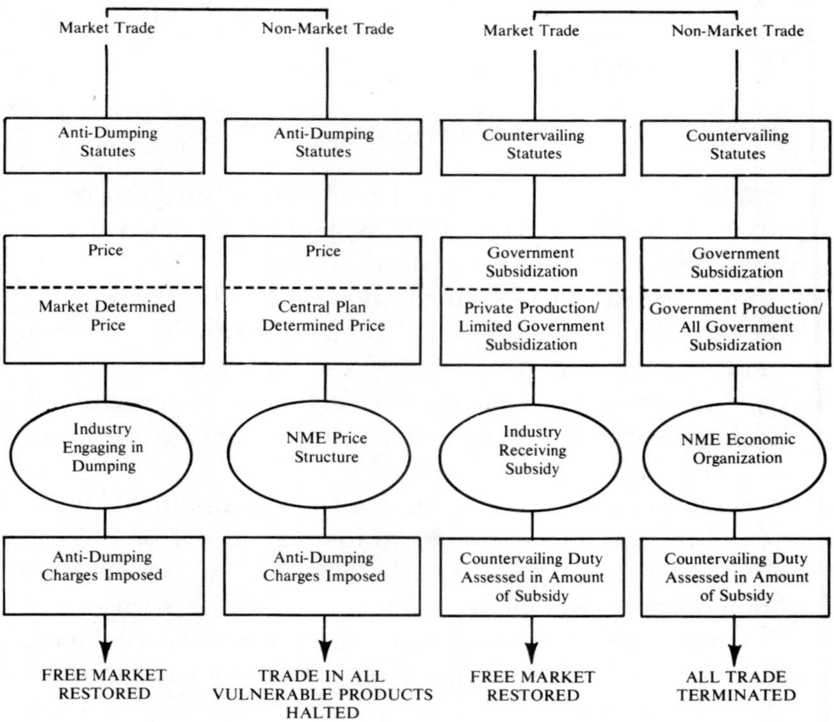

Market Trade
Non-Market Trade
Market Trade
Non-Market Trade
Anti-Dumping Statutes
Anti-Dumping Statutes
Countervailing Statutes
Countervailing Statutes
Price
Market Determined Price
Price
Central Plan Determined Price
Government Subsidization
Private Production/ Limited Government Subsidization
Government Subsidization
Government Production/ All Government Subsidization
Industry Engaging in Dumping
NME Price Structure
Industry Receiving Subsidy
NME Economic Organization
Anti-Dumping Charges Imposed
Anti-Dumping Charges Imposed
Countervailing Duty Assessed in Amount of Subsidy
Countervailing Duty Assessed in Amount of Subsidy
FREE MARKET RESTORED
TRADE IN ALL VULNERABLE PRODUCTS HALTED
FREE MARKET RESTORED
ALL TRADE TERMINATED

raise its export prices or that such trade would be terminated. The situation worsens with countervailing duties. In this case all trade is threatened because virtually all NME economic activity involves subsidization. Nor is it likely that NME economic reforms, no matter how significant, would completely alter this fact of life. The only appropriate safeguard devices are the market disruption clauses, as provided in bilateral agreements and in the Trade Act of 1974, which make an evaluation on the basis of domestic impact alone—not on the basis of the fairness of the trade practice itself.

Discussion and Conclusions

Bilaterals as a Means of Facilitating Trade

When MFN status has been denied, there is no doubt of the value of bilateral agreements to expand trade and harmonize trade practices with a nonmarket economy. However, the stimulative effect of a bilateral instrument cannot approach the stimulative effect of the desire to trade and the economic inducements to trade. The suspicion that economic advantage is the real determinant of trade volume is borne out by most trade statistics, which often record trade increases in the face of political setbacks (see table III-8).

If economic factors are the main determinants of trade, what function does the bilateral instrument perform? First, what the general trade bilateral or economic cooperation bilateral does provide for all parties—market economy or nonmarket economy—is a sense of stability and permanence in the bilateral relationship. And while a long-term, normalized relationship is often emphasized by socialist planners, it is certainly no less critical and may even be more essential to Western firms and businesses seeking to trade with planned economies. The importance of the "blessing" function of bilaterals should not be underestimated. Second, a bilateral agreement enumerates the minimum political and economic conditions required by both parties to maintain regular, long-term, mutually beneficial trade. Third, a bilateral seeks

Table III-8
COMPARISON OF U.S.-SOVIET, -ROMANIAN, -POLISH TRADE PERFORMANCE
(million U.S. $)

	1960	1964	1968	1970	1972	1973	1974	1975
U.S.-Soviet Turnover (exports & imports)	61.20	165.54	114.08	182.37	634.40	1400.85	956.88	2,109.31
U.S. Balance of Trade with the USSR	15.68	123.54	.72	54.07	458.84	973.35	257.84	1,555.91
U.S.-Romanian Turnover (exports & imports)	2.65	6.38	23.75	79.45	98.25	172.21	407.64	343.79
U.S. Balance of Trade with Romania	−.13	3.90	12.63	53.09	39.85	60.81	146.60	34.77
U.S.-Polish Turnover (exports & imports)	181.74	192.07	179.08	167.44	250.76	531.22	660.52	839.77
U.S. Balance of Trade with Poland	104.44	83.75	−14.74	−27.76	−27.70	167.42	128.66	320.30

Source: For 1960-1972 — *First Quarterly Report to the Congress and the East-West Foreign Trade Board on Trade Between the United States and the Nonmarket Economy Countries*, International Trade Commission, March 31, 1975.

For 1973-1975 — *U.S. Trade with Socialist Countries*, Bureau of East-West Trade, Department of Commerce, February 19, 1976.

various means to facilitate trade. Fourth, a bilateral relates its obligations to the obligations of other agreements. And fifth, it can include issues of special and unusual significance for the two parties.

An examination of each different role can provide some assessment of how the bilateral agreement can be used to build a long-term, relatively stable but increasingly beneficial economic relationship. The "blessing function," or door-opening function, is the requisite first step. It is important not only in getting things started but in establishing a firm foundation for future evolution in the relationship. And it contains the implicit guarantee by the respective governments that, at least for the term of the agreement, such economic activity will be viewed with favor.

The second function, establishing minimum conditions necessary to maintain the mutually beneficial aspect of the trade, is essentially an exercise in letting the other side in on the rules of the game. It is a message to the trade partner as to which issues are sensitive and which are not. It is inevitable that the sensitive issues will change over time, and there must be sufficient leeway to adapt to such changes. This second function affects the stability of the relationship and its ability to evolve and continue successfully over time.

However, of all the functions a bilateral can undertake, it is the facilitating function that is most crucial to stimulating the volume and value of trade. The importance of removing obstacles has been borne out by the fact that so many different facilitation issues—trade targets, business, credit, and arbitration facilitation—have been addressed by bilaterals.

The other two functions (relation to other agreements and special areas of interest) are ancillary to the first three. Their raison d'être is to seek solutions to problems (with other obligations or about a specific issue) that might affect or impair the bilateral relationship.

Finally, it is the responsibility of the respective governments to see that the above commitments are maintained—the commitment to the relationship itself, the commitment to the rules, the commitment to remove obstacles, and the commitment to resolve problems. No agreement, regardless of its drafting clarity, can maintain these necessary commitments. Ultimately, business facilitation by the NMEs depends on the performance of state bureaucracies, and the extent of access to Western markets depends on the minimum amount of import protection required by Western governments, industries, and workers. For these reasons bilateral agreements are comparatively weak links relying largely on the relative importance of the particular bilateral relationship to preclude their disruption. The real objective of a bilateral is, given the preexisting political desire to trade and the economic benefits of trade, to find ways to translate that desire into actual transactions and permit the economic dynamics to operate. In the East-West context neither is an easy task because of political differences and economic asymmetries. Nevertheless, it is the general bilateral trade agreement, especially when supplemented by a long-term economic cooperation agreement, that is the most important and effective instrument currently used to encourage and direct East-West commercial relations.

Bilaterals versus Multilaterals

At this point an important distinction should be emphasized. Despite the fact that bilateral agreements are the main instruments for facilitating East-West trade, the actual conduct of East-West trade is becoming increasingly multilateral in nature. That is to say, fewer NME countries are rigidly binding themselves to a system of bilateral trade or payments balances with the Western market economies. Instead, they use foreign exchange earned in one country to pay for imports from another country, or finance deficits by borrowing from external sources. Bilateral trade agreements which include credit provisions and which do *not* require year-to-year bilateral balances increase the multilateralism of trade, to the degree that they increase the volume of that trade. Bilateral trade agreements which are in conformity with the bilateral agreements of other countries also increase the degree of multilateralism in East-West trade.

What, then, is an appropriate division of labor with respect to bilateral agreements and multilateral obligations? First of all, some duplication is both necessary and desirable. A bilateral reinforcing a multilateral commitment is very useful and adds strength to that particular commitment. Secondly, conflicts between the two types of commitments reflect most directly on the effectiveness of the multilateral instrument. They highlight weaknesses and danger areas in the multilateral system. Thirdly, in the absence of effective multilateral commitments with respect to joint production cooperation and business facilitation, these—since they can be a form of NME reciprocation for MFN treatment—should be integral aspects of bilaterals. Finally, certain types of issues are better suited to bilateral instruments (commercial offices, joint commissions), some to multilateral fora (certain nontariff barriers), and some (MFN treatment and market disruption) should be included in both.

The present judgment that bilateral agreements are the most effective instruments in East-West trade is true both because of their obvious advantages and because current multilateral instruments are poor facilitators of East-West trade. Under these conditions, "creative bilateralism" should attempt as one of its goals to establish accommodation mechanisms which later can be multilateralized. It may very well be, given the current political environment, that the multilateral improvements which might be negotiable in the future are the mechanisms which are being explored and developed bilaterally today.

Recommendations

The ability of the bilateral agreement to break new ground rests most directly on its ability to develop new accommodation mechanisms between the two different economic systems. The main problem-solving forum of the bilateral relationship is the joint commission. Most criticism of joint commission work is that it often falls far short of its potential, or worse, that it serves merely as window dressing.

It would appear that the ability of a joint commission to

devise accommodation mechanisms depends on its ability to foresee and circumvent problems arising from the day-to-day conduct of trade and economic relations. The key to achieving this goal is effective monitoring of general trade and economic developments, reinforced by adequate information about new trends, and sufficient flexibility to deal with different problems by a variety of methods. For example, some problems are sufficiently political in nature that they can only be resolved at the ministerial level in periodic high-level conferences. Specific issues such as industrial cooperation can be dealt with by working groups. Ministerial meetings, tied to the calendar and convened to resolve no specific problem, are not particularly useful—especially when they cover the same issues that were covered with another NME a short time before.

A far more difficult problem is that of finding a means of coordinating the policies of the Western countries in East-West trade. Right now the chances for stimulating interest in and effecting such cooperation seem dim. The United States has linked both credits and MFN status to emigration policies. The European Community is trying to establish a common East-West trade policy and define its role in regard to CMEA. The respective positions on market disruption and quotas are disparate. The different business-government relationships in the United States and other industrialized nations are significant factors underlying the differences of approach and factors which are unlikely to change. The United States has unilaterally limited its ability to compete for its share of Eastern markets. Cooperation between competitor nations usually comes about when it becomes clear that competition is disadvantageous to all. With competition unilaterally reduced, the necessity for cooperation is similarly reduced.

If, however, a "gentleman's agreement" on trade bilaterals with the NMEs could be drawn up by the major market economies, what would be its benefits and what form might it take? First, it would constitute a step beyond simple bilateralism toward a multilateral mechanism and by this means give accommodation measures wider currency. Second, if such a "model agreement" reduced barriers on both sides and was not restrictive in nature, it would be likely to stimulate trade to the benefit of all. Third, it would reduce the competitive disadvantages resulting from conflicting national policies. Finally, it would present the NMEs with a more coherent trade policy, and one which was more consistent in its application to East-West trade. Better marketing decisions could then be made both by NME governments and by Western businesses. The OECD has conducted discussions on Western coordination with regard to East-West trade. It would be a suitable forum to begin talks among Western governments on such an agreement, especially while the EC relations with the NMEs remain in limbo.

Such a model bilateral should include all the important issues discussed in this paper—business facilitation, industrial cooperation, credits, nontariff barriers, MFN status, market disruption, and supply access. While U.S. bilaterals, French bilaterals, and German bilaterals have omitted some of the above topics, any standardized bilateral should attempt to address all the major issues. As a second best option, these issues could be handled in "bundles" such as business facilitation and industrial cooperation; credits; nontariff barriers and MFN; market disruption and supply access. Singling out one topic, with the possible exception of credits, could tend to transfer problems from one area into another area and thus be counterproductive. Finally, even if such a comprehensive approach should not prove feasible, exploratory discussions along these lines among East-West trade experts in the respective nations would be most useful in identifying areas for cooperation and coordination, and would be constructive preliminaries to official government negotiations.

Annex B
Select Market Disruption Clauses

The GATT "Escape Clause"

Article XIX: Emergency Action on Imports of Particular Products

1. (a) If, as a result of unforeseen developments and of the effect of the obligations incurred by a contracting party under this Agreement, including tariff concessions, any product is being imported into the territory of that contracting party in such increased quantities and under such conditions as to cause or threaten serious injury to domestic producers in that territory of like or directly competitive products, the contracting party shall be free, in respect of such product, and to the extent and for such time as may be necessary to prevent or remedy such injury, to suspend the obligation in whole or in part or to withdraw or modify the concession.

U.S.-USSR Bilateral of 1972

Article 3

Each Government may take such measures as it deems appropriate to ensure that the importation of products originating in the other country does not take place in such quantities or under such conditions as to cause, threaten or contribute to disruption of its domestic market.

Trade Act of 1974

Section 406: Market Disruption

(a)(1) Upon the filing of a petition by an entity described in section 201(a)(1), upon the request of the President or the Special Representative for Trade Negotiations, upon resolution of either the Committee on Ways and Means of the

House of Representatives or the Committee on Finance of the Senate, or on its own motion, the International Trade Commission (hereafter in this section referred to as the "Commission") shall promptly make an investigation to determine, with respect to imports of an article which is the product of a Communist country, whether market disruption exists with respect to an article produced by a domestic industry.

(e) For purposes of this section—

(1) The term "Communist country" means any country dominated or controlled by communism.

(2) Market disruption exists within a domestic industry whenever imports of an article, like or directly competitive with an article produced by such domestic industry, are increasing rapidly, either absolutely or relatively, so as to be a significant cause of material injury, or threat thereof, to such domestic industry.

United States-Romanian Trade Agreement

Article III: Safeguards

1. The Parties agree to consult promptly at the request of either Party should it determine that actual or prospective imports of products originating in the territory of the other Party are causing or threaten to cause, or are significantly contributing to market disruption within a domestic industry of the requesting Party.

2. Either Party may impose such restrictions as it deems appropriate on imports originating in the territory of the other Party to prevent or remedy such actual or threatened market disruption.

Finnish-Czech Free Trade Agreement

Article 10

1. If the imports of products originating in the territory of one of the Contracting Parties take place in such increased

quantities and/or under such conditions as to cause or threaten to cause disruption to the domestic market or production of the other Contracting Party, the Contracting Party concerned may take, in accordance with the procedures laid down in paragraph 4 of this Article, such measures as is necessary to prevent or remedy the situation.

2. Likewise, such measures may be taken by the Contracting Party concerned if serious disturbances arise in any sector of the economy or if difficulties arise which could cause deterioration in the economic situation of the region.

3. In the selection of measures, priority must be given to those which least disturb the functioning of the Agreement.

4

GATT as a Framework for East-West Trade

John W. Evans

GATT Status of Nonmarket Countries

This chapter rests on the premise that is central to the East-West trade study as a whole: that an increase in peaceful trade between the market economies and the nonmarket economies would have both economic and political value to the United States. When we turn to the question of how best to accomplish such an increase, a further assumption is justified: that the most desirable course, if feasible, would be to act within a multilateral framework, such as the GATT, in order to discourage discrimination and achieve the largest increment in real income.

The central focus will be on the feasibility of such a multilateral approach and the offsetting disadvantages, if any, that it would entail. In this connection the study will examine the experience already acquired as a result of the participation in the GATT of certain Eastern European countries; the constraints imposed by existing economic and political relationships; and the limitations required by existing U.S. legislation. In this examination we will be concerned, inter alia, with the effect that general participation by nonmarket economies in the GATT would have on the continued usefulness of that institution.

Four Eastern European socialist countries (Czechoslovakia, Hungary, Poland, and Romania) are contracting parties to the GATT, but their status differs with respect to the manner in which they achieved that status, with respect to the contents of the instruments under which they achieved it, and, finally, with respect to their GATT relationship with the United States.

Of the four, only one, Czechoslovakia, was a signatory of the original GATT and, therefore, a contracting party by virtue of the 1947 Protocol of Provisional Application.[1] In 1948, while the Havana Conference debating the International Trade Organization Charter Conference was in session, the communist takeover of Czechoslovakia occurred, but Czechoslovakia retained its status as a contracting party. The United States, however, quickly applied its strategic export controls to the new socialist state. Czechoslovakia complained to the contracting parties that the U.S. controls violated its GATT obligations. The case was debated during the Annecy Conference and the Czechoslovakian complaint was rejected (decision of June 8, 1949).[2] In 1951 the U.S. Congress withdrew MFN treatment from the communist bloc, and, at the request of the United States, the contracting parties adopted a declaration granting the two countries the right to suspend their GATT obligations toward each other. No other contracting party followed the U.S. example, and Czechoslovakia has continued, at least nominally, to apply the GATT to all other contracting parties.

The first Eastern European country to accede to the GATT after its formation was Yugoslavia, and while it is not considered a nonmarket economy, the terms of its accession are significant. In 1959 the contracting parties granted Yugoslavia the right to participate in GATT activities until it should consider that it was prepared to assume all the obligations involved in accession (decision of May 25, 1959).[3] At the same Yugoslavia undertook to make the objectives of the GATT a basis for its relations with the other contracting parties, and to apply its provisions "to the extent compatible with its current economic system."

In 1962 Yugoslavia declared itself ready to accede provisionally,[4] subject to the negotiation of its recently adopted customs tariff. It succeeded in convincing a GATT working party that it no longer was a centrally planned economy, that its foreign trade enterprises were now autonomous, and that, as soon as it was in a position to eliminate quantitative restrictions maintained to protect its balance of payments, the tariff would be its only form of import protection. In November 1962 the contracting parties opened for acceptance a declaration granting Yugoslavia provisional contracting party status, pending the completion of tariff negotiations and full accession (declaration of November 13, 1962).[5] In July 1965, Yugoslavia made substantial reductions in its tariff and during the Kennedy Round offered to establish the lower rates as its GATT schedule.[6] Agreement was reached substantially along these lines, and on August 25, 1966, the protocol for Yugoslav accession entered into force.[7] The terms of this protocol were the same as those under which all market economies have acceded and contain none of the special provisions that characterize the protocols of accession of such NMEs as Poland, Romania, or Hungary. Since U.S. legislation exempts Yugoslavia (and Poland) from the discrimination applied to communist countries, U.S. trade relations with Yugoslavia are now governed by the provisions of the GATT.

The remaining Eastern European countries that have become contracting parties have done so under special protocols that recognize the anomaly involved in applying to trade with a nonmarket economy rules that were drawn up on the assumption that trade between participants would generally be conducted by private enterprise and, except where governments intervened, would be influenced primarily by the forces of the profit motive and competition.

Each of these protocols permits other contracting parties "temporarily" to maintain their own discriminatory quantitative restrictions against the acceding country. The differences between these protocols arise in part from the differences in their timing—the Polish protocol was drawn up in 1967, the Romanian in 1971, and the Hungarian in 1973. The greatest differences, however, arise from the fact that Hungary had adopted a customs tariff before its accession, whereas both Poland and Romania, in lieu of tariff concessions, undertook quantitative commitments concerning the level of their imports from the contracting parties as a whole. Each of the three protocols includes a requirement for periodic consultations with the contracting parties concerning its operation. In the following comparisons of the protocols, information derived from these consultations will be drawn upon where relevant.

Import Commitments

Poland undertook to increase its imports from the contracting parties as a whole by 7 percent each year, subject to a renegotiation provision parallel with that which permits contracting parties periodically to renegotiate their tariff schedules. Romania, on the other hand, simply recorded its firm intention of increasing imports from the contracting parties as a whole "at a rate not smaller than the growth of total Romanian imports provided in its five year plans." The Romanian schedule, however, reserves for Romania the right to renegotiate this commitment if it should decide to introduce a customs tariff. Hungary, as indicated above, followed the normal pattern of binding its schedule of tariff concessions to the contracting parties.

The first three annual reviews under the Polish protocol revealed that Poland had exceeded an annual average increase of 7 percent in imports but had not been able to maintain that rate of increase in each individual year over the previous year. During the third review, in 1971, the working party agreed that it was unreasonable to require a 7 percent increase each year over the preceding year and adopted a formula under which Poland's import commitment in any one year would be based on actual imports in 1970 plus a compounded 7 percent annual increase.[8] During the sixth review in 1973, the working party calculated that in 1971 and 1972 together imports from the contracting parties constituted 294 percent of 1970 imports from the contracting parties, "thus considerably exceeding Poland's commitment of 221.5 percent." During the earlier reviews the share of

GATT countries in total Polish imports had shown a slight decline, from 41.8 percent in 1969 to 41 percent in 1970. But in 1971 the percentage rose to 43.9 percent and in 1972 to 49.2 percent.

The first review under the Romanian protocol occurred too early to permit a determination as to whether Romanian imports from the contracting parties would keep pace with total imports under the five-year plan. However, Romania has since notified the contracting parties of its intention to adopt a customs tariff and, as permitted by the protocol, to substitute a tariff schedule for its quantitative import commitment. The new tariff has been under intensive examination in a GATT working party. In spite of the invocation by the United States of Article XXXV of the GATT[9] at the time of Romanian accession, the United States is a member and active participant in the working party. This has been possible because the U.S.-Romanian bilateral agreement, concluded in April 1975, provided that the parties would apply between themselves the provisions of the GATT and the Romanian protocol of accession (for a description of this bilateral agreement see the section on dumping in this chapter).

Since the Hungarian tariff was accepted in its protocol of accession, import commitments were not necessary.

Maintenance of Discriminatory Quantitative Restrictions by Contracting Parties

The Polish protocol provided that contracting parties might temporarily maintain existing discriminatory quantitative restrictions (QRs)[10] against imports from Poland, but that the discriminatory element in those QRs should not be increased and should be phased out by the end of a transitional period, the terminal date for which was to be established later by agreement.

The Romanian protocol contained a similar provision but proclaimed the "objective" of phasing out discriminatory QRs by the end of 1974, and allowed for the establishment of a later date if elimination had not then been achieved.

The Hungarian protocol established January 1, 1975, as the target date for termination of discriminatory QRs but, as in the case of Romania, provided only that, if any such restrictions were still in force on that date, a working party should "examine them with a view to their elimination."

Only the Polish protocol has been in force long enough to permit a judgment concerning the effectiveness of the commitment by contracting parties to phase out their discriminatory QRs. In terms of the number of countries maintaining any such QRs against Polish imports, it appears that no progress has been made since the first review in 1968. At the time of the first review of the operation of the protocol, thirteen countries notified the contracting parties that they still maintained such restrictions. Five years later, during the sixth review, no country had ended them. All of the European countries that had reported the existence of such restrictions at the time of the first review still maintained them, if the notification by the European Community in the last review is taken to apply to all of its members. In addition to the EC, Austria, Finland, Norway, Sweden, and Switzerland (all of which had notified originally) still maintained some restrictions and had not agreed to a firm date for their termination. Some progress had been made in the liberalization by some countries of certain items, but statements by the contracting parties during the review suggest that these ameliorations were the result of periodic renegotiation under bilateral agreements that each of the countries maintained with Poland. The conclusion seems inescapable that those countries whose trade before Poland's accession was governed by bilateral agreements have continued to depend on such agreements, reinforced by quantitative restrictions, as the way to ensure Polish imports of their goods.

Escape Clause and Withdrawal

The Polish protocol contains an escape clause benefiting the other contracting parties—but not Poland—which is substantially easier to use than Article XIX, the general escape clause of the GATT. In the event of serious injury or threat of injury to a domestic industry, the contracting party concerned, after due notice and consultation, may take unilateral action against the imports concerned. In contrast to the provisions of Article XIX, the increased imports giving rise to the injury need not result from obligations incurred under the agreement, and the restrictions may be applied against Polish trade on a non-MFN basis.

Reinforcing the escape clause, the protocol permits any contracting party, after consultation and negotiation, to suspend any or all of its commitments affecting trade between it and Poland. In this case, Poland is granted the same privilege in its trading relationship with any other contracting party. This privilege goes substantially beyond that in the Protocol of Provisional Application (by whose terms contracting parties have acceded to GATT), under which a contracting party may withdraw from the agreement in toto, but not from its GATT relations with another individual party.

The Romanian and Hungarian protocols contain escape clauses similar to that applying to Poland, but with a difference that is important, at least from the point of view of external appearances: Romania and Hungary are granted the same special escape clause facilities as the other contracting parties. Both protocols also contain the mutual right of suspension included in the Polish protocol.

The special escape clause in the Polish protocol illustrates the fact that, when Poland acceded, the contracting parties were genuinely concerned that Poland might flood their markets, whereas Poland was anxious to accede and refrained from demanding equal rights. In several years of experience with Polish accession, however, no contracting party has invoked the escape clause or suspended its GATT obligations. By the time Romania and Hungary acceded, this fact, as well as political motivations for admitting the latter countries to GATT, enabled them to obtain terms which, at least nominally, were more favorable than Poland's.

Dumping

The working party that negotiated the Polish protocol was concerned as to how the limitations in Article VI of the GATT on the imposition of antidumping duties could be interpreted in the case of exports from a country where domestic prices were under state control and did not necessarily have any relationship to production costs. The working party was aided by the existence of the second interpretative note to paragraph 1 of Article VI, which deals with this situation.[11] In view of that note, the working party was able to omit any reference to the problem in the protocol itself, but recorded in its report that the note would apply to exports from Poland and that "a Contracting Party may use as the normal value for a product imported from Poland the prices which prevail normally in its market," or, alternatively, "a price constructed on the basis of a like product originating in another country."

The working party on accession of Romania recorded a similar understanding in its report. The report of the working party on Hungary's accession included identical language concerning the action that might be taken by contracting parties but omitted any reference to the interpretative note as the legal basis for that conclusion. This omission was presumably intentional, possibly arising from an objection by Hungary to the reference in that note to "a country where all domestic prices are fixed by the state."

Neither the annual reviews under the Polish protocol nor the record of the first Romanian review indicates that these provisions have been invoked by any contracting party.

Most-Favored-Nation Status

With the exception noted below for Hungary, the protocols for the accession of all three countries incorporate the general MFN commitments of the GATT without singling them out for special reference. This is qualified, of course, by the facilities granted the other contracting parties with respect to certain discriminatory QRs. The most important qualification, however, is in paragraph 3 of the Hungarian protocol, which stipulates that the incorporation of the GATT provisions shall not prevent Hungary from maintaining its "existing trading regulations" with respect to products of the CMEA countries listed in Annex A of the protocol.

Although the working party reports do not throw any light on why a similar provision was not included in the Polish and Romanian protocols, it is logical to assume that, in the absence of a customs tariff, these countries did not find it necessary to admit that they practiced discrimination in favor of CMEA members.

International Political Constraints

Officials of international organizations believe almost unanimously that the idea of simultaneous participation in the GATT by both the USSR and the other Eastern European countries is visionary. The reasons given include a conviction that the USSR would never accept the qualified terms of GATT membership already included in the accession protocols of Poland, Romania, and Hungary; the differences between the trading systems of the NMEs; and, above all, the opposition of many Eastern European countries to the establishment of a uniform set of rules for East-West trade in a multilateral agreement in which they and the USSR would be partners. Eastern European officials confirm this view, emphasizing especially the differences among the trading systems of the NMEs.

A multilateral trade agreement in East-West trade implies uniformity of treatment by the United States of the NMEs included in the agreement. It also implies a degree of unanimity among the NMEs themselves as to the distance they are willing to go in meeting U.S. demands—demands to which other U.S. trading partners are not subjected. If the USSR were a member, it would almost certainly set the limits to which it is willing to go and to which it would permit its CMEA partners to go, and it is hardly a remote possibility that these limits would conform to the requirements of the Trade Act of 1974.

U.S. Legislative Constraints

The Trade Act of 1974 imposes serious limitations on any trade agreement with nonmarket economies, especially on the extension of MFN treatment, without which a worthwhile agreement would be impossible to achieve.[12] The following analysis will examine the problems that would arise in the negotiation and implementation of agreements under the 1974 Trade Act. But it will first deal with the antecedent question of whether the act, by intention or design, rules out GATT relations or other multilateral relations between the United States and NMEs, either singly or collectively.

Under the 1974 Trade Act, the president is denied the power to grant MFN status to an NME not already entitled to such treatment, i.e., to any NME except Poland or Yugoslavia,[13] unless he has first negotiated a "bilateral commercial agreement" which conforms to a number of explicit requirements and which has been approved by both houses of Congress.

There can be no question that the requirement of a bilateral agreement was intended to prevent the administration from using the accession of an NME to the GATT as the occasion for granting to the NME most-favored-nation treatment. The report of the Congressional Conference Committee which negotiated the differences between the House bill and the Senate bill makes it clear that the committee had intentionally rejected a provision in the House bill that would have permitted the president to extend MFN status to an NME if the NME and the United States were to become parties to a multilateral agreement meeting certain specifications. Both the text of the 1974 Trade Act and this legislative history also rule out the extension of MFN status through a multilateral agreement other than the GATT.

Under the Trade Act, it is not possible for the President to initiate MFN treatment through a bilateral agreement and then terminate the bilateral and substitute for it a multilateral agreement calling for the continuation of MFN, for the Trade Act explicitly requires the termination of MFN treatment if the bilateral is terminated (Sec. 404[b]).

In theory, the Trade Act permits the conclusion of bilateral agreements with NMEs for periods up to three years, renewable for similar periods. In practice, however, the requirements of Section 402 for periodic congressional review of emigration policies limit the duration of MFN status (after an initial period of up to eighteen months) to a year-to-year basis. MFN treatment could be cut off from any NME by the failure of either house of Congress, on the occasion of such a review, to approve a presidential recommendation for extension. Under these circumstances the termination of MFN status (and therefore of the agreement) would take place immediately, without provision for advance notice. There is no provision of the GATT that would permit a contracting party to terminate its relations with one other party unless it withdraws totally from the GATT. And even this withdrawal, under the Protocol of Provisional Application, requires a sixty-day prior notice. The Trade Act further requires that a bilateral with an NME contain—

1. a provision that would permit the United States to take any action it considers necessary for reasons of national security (the corresponding GATT provision is limited to trade in arms for a military establishment and fissionable materials, unless the action is taken "in time of war or other emergency in international relations" [Article XXI]); and
2. an escape clause for "market disruption" based on criteria considerably easier to meet than the criteria specified in the Trade Act for escape clause action against non-NMEs and easier than either those in Article XIX of the GATT or in the Romanian and Polish protocols.

In taking action under the escape clause stipulated in the Trade Act, the president may not apply the action on an MFN basis as required by the GATT.

The Trade Act is ambiguous on the question of whether

the president is empowered to exercise the tariff-cutting power granted him in the act in an agreement with an NME. If the intention was to rule out tariff negotiations with NMEs, the United States would be unable to participate in a GATT negotiation for full accession of any NME which should choose, like Hungary—and now Romania—to adopt a customs tariff for negotiating purposes. If the intention was to permit such negotiations but to subject them, like the other elements of a bilateral, to approval by both houses of Congress, a meaningful negotiation would be impracticable. Even when the administration acts under a qualified delegation of authority, the negotiation of tariff concessions is complex and difficult. It is doubtful that any country would be willing to negotiate circumstances under which the agreement could be upset by congressional disapproval of even a single concession.

These requirements compound the impossibility of meeting the requirements of the Trade Act within the framework of the GATT or any other multilateral agreement.

In addition to direct conflicts with the GATT, the requirements for a bilateral under the Trade Act include provisions for which the GATT contains no counterpart and which have never been considered to be within its purview, for example, commitments regarding services; protection of patents, trademarks, and copyrights; participation in trade fairs; and facilities for commercial representatives.

From the analysis so far, two conclusions seem inescapable. (1) There is no chance of negotiating terms of accession to the GATT of even one NME that would reflect the legislative requirements for a bilateral. (2) The United States could accept the accession of an NME only if its bilateral with that country were to stipulate that any conflict between it and the GATT, as modified by the protocol of accession, would be resolved in favor of the bilateral.

The U.S.-Romanian Bilateral Agreement

The conclusion in the preceding section, based on an analysis of the Trade Act, is borne out by the bilateral agreement concluded between the United States and Romania in April 1975 and subsequently approved by both houses of Congress. Specifically, in order to avoid conflict with the Trade Act, the agreement, while incorporating those provisions of the GATT that are not in conflict with the bilateral, explicitly provides that to the extent that any provisions of the GATT are inconsistent with the provisions of the bilateral, the latter shall apply.

The bilateral agreement contains a number of provisions not relevant to the GATT but required by the Trade Act, having to do with business facilitation, protection of industrial property and copyrights, facilities for payments, navigation, and governmental commercial offices. Otherwise, the principal provisions that differ from the GATT, as modified by the accession protocol, are:

1. *Escape clause.* Both parties have the right, after consultation, to take such action as they consider necessary to combat market disruption caused by imports from the other. No provision is made for the notification of, or the receipt of recommendations from, the GATT contracting parties.
2. *Trade commitments.* In lieu of the quantitative commitment in Romania's protocal of accession, both parties "envision" that total bilateral trade will at least triple during the initial three-year period of the agreement.
3. *National security.* The requirement of the Trade Act that bilaterals must include an exception for national security is met by a provision in the agreement to the effect that either party has the right to take any action for the protection of its security interests.

Discussion and Conclusions

There is one respect in which the GATT experience favors the use of that organization as a framework for governing trade relations with the NMEs: it has proved possible to use GATT accession as a means of establishing continuing consultations between an NME and the contracting parties.

On the other hand, there is little in that experience to suggest that GATT membership has led the NMEs to alter their trading systems or to reduce the role played by state decisions in determining the flow of trade.

The fact that Poland has more than met its quantitative import commitments does not affect this judgment. Granted a desire on Poland's part to increase her trade with the West, a 7 percent annual increase would almost certainly have occurred even under more stable monetary conditions. But in the light of the inflation that has prevailed during most of the course of her membership, a failure to meet that goal would have required a positive effort on her part to reduce the share of the contracting parties in her total trade.

A detailed examination of the development of the trade of each NME since its accession and a comparison with the trade of non-GATT NMEs would be of interest, but would have limited diagnostic value. Even if such a study should show that the trade of acceders with contracting parties has grown more rapidly than that of nonacceders, this need not be the result of adherence to the rules of GATT. Those NMEs interested in GATT accession have been motivated by a desire to increase their trade with the West and almost certainly would have increased their imports in response to any increase in their exports to GATT countries, whatever the cause of that increase. The decisive motivation of Poland, Romania, and Hungary for seeking GATT status has been the desire to obtain assured MFN treatment. In spite of the discriminatory QRs that remain, accession probably has contributed to the reduction in discrimination against their exports, and thus indirectly to the increase in their imports from contracting parties. But similar increases would probably have occurred if MFN treatment had been unilaterally granted, or granted in bilateral agreements.

The previous chapter on the conduct of East-West trade by the nonmarket economies indicates a trend toward some liberal reform by the NMEs. But the question remains to what degree the GATT NMEs are in fact converting their systems in the direction of substituting competition for fiat as the determinant of trade flows; for example, whether the

Hungarian tariff is that country's sole remaining instrument for interfering with imports. The contracting parties tacitly accepted the Hungarian assertion to that effect, but available records do not establish whether they did so because they had solid evidence to support it or because of their politically motivated desire to receive Hungary as a contracting party on terms she would accept.

The increasing lenience in the terms the contracting parties have imposed on acceding NMEs derives in part from the same dominance of international politics over the earlier desire to preserve the integrity of the rules of the GATT. This change of emphasis, in turn, is related to the general decline in the credibility of the GATT contract, which has been discussed in detail in a recent study by the Atlantic Council of the United States, *GATT Plus*. But it also suggests the danger that a movement to bring still more NMEs into the GATT framework may contribute toward "GATTerdämmerung." The experience so far with the membership of a few NMEs in the GATT not only leaves substantial doubt that any economic ends have been served but raises the possibility that general NME membership would be costly to the aim of orderly trading relationships among the existing contracting parties.

The GATT is essentially a multilateral contract, administered by the contracting parties and lacking either a strong executive or sovereign powers to enforce its rules. Its effectiveness depends on the confidence each contracting party has that the parties in general will interpret those rules from a similar perspective and be guided by them. Until quite recently the provisions of the agreement have generally been interpreted in the context of the trading systems of most of the members, in which the major determinant of trade flows is competition and in which governmental intervention, when it occurs, is plainly visible. The tariff, as the principal instrument of such interventions, is subject to limitation by negotiation, and, under the GATT, may be supplemented by specified nontariff barriers only in special circumstances, which are themselves defined.

When the commonly accepted interpretations of the

GATT rules are weakened by serious departures from this standard trading system, the entire fabric of the contract is threatened. A contracting party that is tempted to ignore the rules in a particular case finds it easier to do so if such key concepts as nondiscrimination and unimpeded access to markets, having lost their earlier precision, have been successfully ignored by others.

The recent protocols of accession of NMEs have debased the meaning of many of the key elements in the multilateral contract. Most-favored-nation treatment cannot have the same meaning when applied to the trade decisions of an NME as it does when the nature and extent of governmental intervention are determined by law and regulation. Given the trend in the latest protocols to gloss over the differences in trading systems, the process of debasement appears to be accelerating. In order to obtain the nominal adherence of the remaining NMEs, especially the USSR, any remaining precision in the original meaning of the GATT concepts would almost surely have to be sacrificed.

Even if this danger did not exist, any plan for using the GATT as the framework for regulating trade relations with NMEs would have to overcome formidable practical obstacles. One of these obstacles could be surmounted if the contracting parties were to abandon all efforts to restore the effectiveness of the GATT as a contract and retreat to regarding it solely as a forum for consultation. But it might still be impossible to obtain the cooperation of those Eastern European countries which have an aversion to joint membership with the USSR. And the Soviet Uion itself is unlikely to see any advantage in participation that does not guarantee her unqualified MFN status in Western markets.

While some contracting parties might be willing to grant Moscow such unrequited benefits, the constraints imposed by the Trade Act of 1974 on the U.S. president would preclude U.S. participation unless the executive branch should seek and obtain drastic amendments to the law. Some amendments, to make the law conform more closely to the country's real economic interests, may be possible. But any administration seeking changes that would permit it to use the GATT, or any other multilateral organization, as a framework for trade relations with the NMEs as a group will have to be able to provide assurances of a greater measure of reciprocity than now seems possible.

5

The Tokyo Round and the Nonmarket Economies: A Focus on Nontariff Barriers

Karen C. Taylor

A major activity of the General Agreement on Tariffs and Trade (GATT) has been to conduct rounds of tariff liberalizing negotiations. The seventh such round was initiated in Tokyo in September 1973 and got under way in Geneva in February 1975. The Tokyo Round of multilateral trade negotiations is unique. Previous rounds of trade negotiations focused mainly on the problem of reducing tariffs. For example, the preceding round of negotiations, the Kennedy Round (1963-1967), was generally successful in reducing tariffs and achieved on average a reduction of about 35 percent on industrial goods. However, the Kennedy Round, despite the negotiation of an antidumping code, failed to deal comprehensively with nontariff barriers or trade in agricultural products.

In contrast, the negotiators of the Tokyo Round will tackle not only the problem of reducing tariffs, but also questions concerning the reform of GATT and nontariff barriers to trade. The Tokyo Round also differs from previous rounds in that it is the first such negotiation to open its doors to non-GATT members. It is in effect a negotiation among those who agree to negotiate.

Like the GATT itself, the Tokyo Round of trade negotiations is principally concerned with harmonizing relations among its negotiating parties. The broad question of how best to regulate and facilitate trade between market and nonmarket economies (NMEs) will not arise. However, six nonmarket countries (Bulgaria, Cuba, Czechoslovakia, Hungary, Poland, and Romania) are participating in the multilateral trade negotiations (MTN) and will have an opportunity to provide inputs to and to benefit from any liberalization that is achieved.[1]

Despite the fact that the MTN will not prove to be an exceptionally suitable vehicle for examining the general framework of East-West trade relations, it will address specific issues of relevance to East-West trade. Further, since bilateral trade agreements with almost all the Western European nations and the question of most-favored-nation (MFN) status with the United States remain active issues, participation in the MTN by the NMEs will affect their bilateral relations with Western nations, a much more significant factor in NME trade than their GATT obligations.

The following presentation examines the issues which will be discussed in the MTN and which are of greatest relevance to East-West trade. The purpose is to examine the question of what constitutes meaningful reciprocity in the context of the negotiations, and to sketch some recommendations for the MTN which could lead to an improved ability to deal multilaterally with trade between market and nonmarket economies.

The negotiations have been subdivided into six working groups, on nontariff barriers, tropical products, tariffs, agriculture, industrial sector negotiations, and safeguards. While the tropical-products and industrial-sector negotiations will be of specific value to specific NME countries, the issues of general and primary importance with respect to the structure of East-West trade are nontariff barriers, safeguards, agriculture, and tariffs. The nontariff group itself has been broken down into five subgroups, on technical barriers to trade (standards), subsidies and countervailing duties, quantitative restrictions, customs matters, and government procurement.

With numerous subgroups and various bilateral and

multilateral consultations on many of the issues taking place, this is a very full plate indeed. It can be argued that the introduction of East-West issues could overload the negotiators and jeopardize the success of the MTN. On the other hand, six NMEs are already participating, and reciprocity must be sought for tariff concessions. The opportunity exists to discuss with NME representatives specific issues and, in the context of these issues, relevant differences between market and nonmarket economies. Finally, the NMEs have an interest in improving their status through the negotiations, which gives the Western nations a certain degree of negotiating leverage. The risk to the MTN would in any case be limited since those East-West issues which might threaten the success of the general negotiations would surely be dropped by the Western nations and could not be forced to conclusion by the NMEs. Complete avoidance of East-West issues by the Tokyo Round would merely continue an already prolonged silence on matters that will have an increasing influence on the structure of world trade.

Nontariff Barriers

As the preceding rounds of tariff negotiations have achieved a significant reduction in the level of tariffs, nontariff barriers have taken on greater importance.[2] In the decade of 1965-1975, governments have become more active in such areas as environment and consumer protection and have enacted regulations which have an impact on the world economy and international trade patterns. New nontariff barriers have arisen in this fashion. It is precisely the fact that nontariff barriers are national legislative responses to internal and very often legitimate needs that makes it difficult to negotiate multilateral solutions.

Some 800 different nontariff barriers have been catalogued in trade among the Western nations. No systematic effort has been made to categorize the nontariff barriers presented by NMEs. (The old saw that a nonmarket economy is just one big nontariff barrier may have a good deal of truth in it, but it is scarcely helpful in terms of analyzing obstacles and suggesting remedies.) Since tariffs play an extremely limited role in determining trade flows to nonmarket economies, nontariff barriers certainly are a major concern.

Despite the vastness of the problem and the difficulties in reaching solutions in this field, it is precisely in the area of nontariff barriers that some progress is possible in the MTN. The reasons for this are threefold: (1) the diversity of nontariff barriers being considered presents some prime targets for solution; (2) nations are more politically motivated to control the nontariff barrier problem than they were in the past; and (3) in several areas, especially those unrelated to price, NMEs would not necessarily require differential treatment.

The main nontariff barriers discussed in this paper are standards, subsidies and countervailing duties, antidumping regulations, safeguards, and quantitative restrictions. Some major nontariff barriers not discussed here are government procurement, customs matters, discriminatory bilateral agreements, shipping regulations, and special duties on imports.[3]

Standards

Standards include such practices as health, safety, and industrial standards, as well as labeling and processing requirements. A GATT working party has been examining the question of standards since 1971 and has completed a draft code of behavior. The Economic Commission for Europe has also completed work on a draft code of standards definitions, and both drafts are being considered by the MTN standards group as the basis for their discussions. Because standards issues tend to be universal and do not relate differently to market and nonmarket structures, because a centralized authority is better equipped to implement a standards code, because the harmonization of standards is mutually advantageous, and because so much prior work has already been done, it is quite likely that the MTN will result in a standards code which includes the NMEs.

Briefly, the draft GATT standards code would establish a

series of agreements for the development of mandatory and voluntary standards by central and local governments and for the development of voluntary standards by private bodies. It further provides for methods of determining conformity (certification acceptance procedures) and of coordinating quality assurance systems, establishes groundwork for a standards information system, and provides assistance to developing countries and adherents to the code in matters of compliance. The objectives are to encourage participation in standard writing and certification procedures, eliminate the domestic protection afforded by standards, and avoid third-country injury from any regional standards arrangements. Wherever appropriate, standards are to be specified in terms of performance rather than design.

The MTN standards subgroup has agreed that the standards code would be open to all countries of the world regardless of their GATT or MTN status. A standards code would be potentially attractive to many countries, including especially the NMEs. Since East-West trade is just in the takeoff stage, it would be in the interest of the NMEs to participate in a standards code and thereby obtain the benefits of marketing conformity early in the game.

As to standards in the NME countries, it is difficult to know how many and how important the practices are. It is even more difficult to know how deeply these practices are embedded in the politics of interbureaucratic rivalry. However, work on intra-CMEA (Council for Mutual Economic Assistance) standardization of products and processes has been an established goal of CMEA at least since the late 1950s, and is reflected in the work of various commissions and institutes. In 1975 CMEA set the goal of establishing some 25,000 intra-CMEA standards, which suggests that this process is already relatively far advanced.

That a commitment to international cooperation on standards is highly possible is implied by the statements on standards contained in the Final Act of the Conference on Security and Cooperation (CSCE) signed in Helsinki on August 1, 1975:

> *The Participating States,*
>
> Recognizing the development of international harmonization of standards and technical regulations and of international co-operation in the field of certification as an important means of eliminating technical obstacles to international trade and industrial co-operation, thereby facilitating their development and increasing productivity;
>
> reaffirm their interest to achieve the widest possible international harmonization of standards and technical regulations;
>
> express their readiness to promote international agreements and other appropriate arrangements on acceptance of certificates of conformity with standards and technical regulations;
>
> consider it desirable to increase international co-operation on standardization, in particular by supporting the activities of intergovernmental and other appropriate organizations in this field.

Despite the significant degree of mutuality, there is some asymmetry involved in the area of standards. When the regulatory body is nongovernmental, a standard is considered voluntary and requires only the "best efforts" of the national government to ensure its enforcement. A mandatory standard applies when the governmental body is the regulatory agency, and it requires "all possible means" to assure its compliance. Because the West in general, and the United States in particular, relies much more heavily on independent groups of experts for their standards regulations, any harmonization efforts would fall more heavily on the shoulders of the NMEs.

Another important aspect of the standards code is the establishment of an information base. The GATT standards code would require proper publication of all standards, details of test methods and administrative procedures, prepublication of new and changed rules, etc. Given the commitment made at the CSCE in Helsinki to improve the quality and quantity of economic and commercial information generally, it would seem that standards information is an area where progress would be possible and where lack of progress would tend to demonstrate a degree of recalcitrance—not only with regard to standards but also with regard to the provision of information in general.

In sum, then, the negotiating aspects for the standards code are that (1) it is possible, (2) it would be mutually beneficial, (3) it falls a bit more directly in its implementation on the NMEs than on the Western countries, and (4) it could provide a test case for the exchange-of-information issue.

Subsidies and Countervailing Duties

An area which illustrates the problems posed by the differences in the two economic systems is the question of subsidies.[4] Very briefly, Western economic theory holds that all subsidies have potential trade-distorting effects. The GATT articles recognize this principle, require notification of subsidy practices by the contracting parties, and provide for consultations. Article XVI describes (but does not define) a domestic subsidy as follows: "any subsidy, including any form of income or price support, which operates directly or indirectly to increase exports of any product from, or to reduce imports of any product into, its territory." GATT has moved more strongly against export subsidies on nonprimary products and, to a lesser degree, primary products than it has against domestic subsidies. However, barring the rather slim guidelines that a subsidy must involve a cost to the government, that subsidies on the export of primary products should be avoided or at least "shall not . . . result in . . . more than an equitable share of world trade in that product," and that export subsidies on industrial products shall cease "which result in the sale . . . for export at a price lower than . . . the comparable price . . . in the domestic market," no exact definitions of either a subsidy or an export subsidy are provided in the GATT articles.

It is useful to examine a 1960 GATT working party report which included an illustrative list of subsidy practices and to relate that list to what is considered to be normal NME behavior. The list includes such items as currency retention schemes with bonuses for exporters; direct subsidies to exporters; the remission of direct taxes related to export; the exemption for exports from indirect taxes greater than those charged on such goods when consumed internally; export credits which do not cover long-term costs or losses; export credits at rates lower than the rates of obtaining such funds in the domestic market; and governments bearing all or part of the costs of obtaining export credits.[5]

This working party also reported on those instances when "any form of income or price support" could be considered to be a subsidy. It members concluded that price support systems maintained by purchases or resales at a loss to the government were subsidies, but that price support systems maintained by quantitative restrictions, flexible tariffs, or similar methods might not be subsidies. Nevertheless, they requested the contracting parties to notify the GATT Secretariat in all cases of price support systems.

Clearly, general subsidies, export subsidies, and price support schemes are provided by the NMEs. Subsidies and export subsidies or similar practices are no doubt necessary, given an economic system which requires imports both for growth sectors and to fill planning gaps, and which tends toward bilateral balancing in the absence of currency convertibility. The resulting view is usually that exports must pay for imports with hard currency.

The traditional method that NMEs used to conduct foreign trade was to buy imports and sell exports at world market prices and charge the consumer the domestic price (which would in effect mean the imposition of a large tax) or pay the producer the domestic price (which usually involved a substantial subsidy). This practice has been altered in recent years by such devices as permitting the enterprises to retain portions of their hard-currency earnings, by attempts to bring domestic prices into closer alignment with efficiency quotients and world prices, and by permitting greater autonomy to enterprises engaging in foreign trade. Hungary has led the way in these reforms. Significant efforts have also been made to promote exports even in the more conservative countries such as the Soviet Union. The net result has probably been to reduce the extent of domestic production subsidies in the NMEs and to increase the extent of export subsidies. The paradox here is that while these foreign trade reforms are certainly a trend toward decentralization and more efficient economic activity for the NMEs, and as such should be regarded as beneficial, in terms of current GATT regulations export subsidies are regarded with much less favor than general subsidies.

The appropriate response to a subsidy is to impose a countervailing duty. A countervailing duty is a special duty to offset the effects of a subsidy and must be an amount equal to that of the subsidy. Countervailing duties can become important nontariff barriers to trade when the country imposing them does not accurately evaluate the effect of the foreign subsidy. Further, GATT regulations (Article VI) require that material injury to the domestic industry (or the material retardation of establishment of a domestic industry) must be determined before a countervailing duty can be imposed. U.S. legislation requires no proof of injury. The U.S. countervailing duty provisions were written in 1897 and were thereby exempt by application of the grandfather clause from conformity with the GATT.

The absence of an injury requirement increases the risk that the application of a countervailing duty will become a disruptive nontariff barrier. This takes on even greater significance when applied to NMEs where the government is the sole agent of economic activity, where subsidization practices are commonplace, where the difficulty of measuring a subsidy is increased because of government secrecy policies with regard to economic data, and where internal prices do not reflect cost/efficiency ratios as in market countries.

A controversial three-tiered system for dealing with subsidies was proposed by the U.S. delegation to the MTN in late 1975. The first tier would include prohibited practices which result in dual pricing, such as direct subsidies for exporters. At this level, no injury requirements would be necessary to impose a countervailing duty. The second tier would deal with domestic subsidies, such as agricultural programs, where proof of injury would be required to countervail and countervailing would be discretionary, not mandatory. The third tier would include acceptable practices such as trade-fair promotion, which could not be countervailed against under any circumstances. Attached to this three-tiered system would be a series of agreements on the various practices, which would outline certain circumstances whereby a second-level practice could be dealt with either as a first-level practice or a third-level practice—in other words circumstances which would move a practice out of its normal category.

Progress in dealing with the problem of subsidies and countervailing duties may occur in the MTN, although the difficulty of these issues for the Western nations may serve to limit actual results. However, what emerges in terms of defining subsidies will no doubt have limited relevance for the NMEs, because market-derived definitions have little connection with economic reality in the NMEs. A more useful course would be to ask what forms of subsidization by the NMEs have the most direct impact on the foreign trade sector, which of these affect world trading competitiveness most adversely, and which cannot be readily compensated for by normal market mechanisms.

To date, scattered complaints about Soviet subsidized shipping, about exports of subsidized agricultural products, and about unfair competition in third markets, especially developing countries, have not been systematically gathered and evaluated using the above criteria. In the absence of such preparatory work it seems unrealistic to expect the MTN to grapple with these issues. What the MTN delegates could usefully do, however, would be to sponsor investigations along the lines suggested above. The object would be to identify and perhaps rank some of the more disruptive NME practices, with an eye to eventually negotiating with the NMEs for their reduction.

Antidumping

Antidumping duties, like countervailing duties, can be significant nontariff barriers to trade. While not currently on the agenda for the multilateral trade negotiations, proposals have been made that a subgroup on antidumping be established. A multilateral Antidumping Code was negotiated in 1966. For domestic legal reasons, the United States need not act strictly in accordance with that code. U.S. nonconformity would be the main topic for discussion between the United States and its trade partners, should the subject arise. But there is a very important aspect affecting trade with NMEs that could also be raised.

Dumping results when an export is sold in the foreign market at a price lower than that for similar transactions made in the domestic market. Given the arbitrary price structures of the NMEs, this poses an almost impossible problem. The practice in the past has been to construct a price based on a third-country production price to serve as the equivalent of the NME domestic price. Particularly when a market economy is used as the basis for comparison, however, the system tends to work in a highly arbitrary fashion. The use of the third-country–price solution in the case of Polish golf cars imported into the United States pointed up major difficulties in applying antidumping regulations to NMEs. Since some NMEs have expressed grave concern regarding the application of existing U.S. antidumping procedures as a means to bar market access for their products, there may be some interest on the part of participating NMEs in bringing up the price construction issue should an antidumping group be organized.

In the case of NMEs, antidumping and countervailing issues are closely intertwined. This is not hard to understand when one considers that these two GATT provisions were designed to take care of the same problem—unfair competition arising from private sector actions (dumping) and public sector actions (subsidization). The mechanisms for dealing with subsidies and dumping have little meaning when applied to the NMEs, and this is one of several reasons why special safeguard provisions have been negotiated in bilateral agreements. It would be most useful to be able to improve the multilateral institutional mechanism for both antidumping and countervailing. In fact, effective multilateralization with respect to special conditions for the NMEs will become necessary if East-West trade increases and brings with it an increased incidence of antidumping and countervailing duties invoked on NME exports.

Safeguards

Another insurance against damaging imports in the GATT system is the safeguard or escape clause, Article XIX. The intent of Article XIX is to protect against the adverse impact of increased imports arising for unforeseen reasons from negotiated trade concessions or other trade obligations. The difficulties with Article XIX are numerous and controversial. A European Community statement sets out the problem of revising the safeguard system:

> It must . . . be recognized that this article has proved difficult to operate effectively and the Community is prepared to take part in any efforts to try and establish a better practical application of the safeguard clause. While the Community favors a more flexible application of this clause than hitherto, this should not have as result that there would be excessive recourse to safeguard measures.[6]

The net result of a general reluctance on the part of the contracting parties to use the escape clause has been to turn increasingly to "voluntary export controls"[7]; the continued maintenance of quantitative restrictions; and an increased use of other nontariff barriers, including antidumping and countervailing duties, to serve the needs of domestic industries for protection.

In East-West trade an additional need for protection has traditionally been perceived. This is based on political differences, but also on the obvious economic differences.

For these reasons, differing safeguard protocols and market disruption provisions have been included in bilateral agreements between market and nonmarket economies. For example, the U.S. market disruption provisions apply more lenient criteria for injury definitions than the GATT escape clause and allow such actions to be taken on a non-MFN basis. (See the U.S.-Romanian Trade Agreement of 1975 and Section 406 of the Trade Act of 1974.)

It is interesting to ask what types of safeguards are better suited to deal with disruptions from NMEs. First, there appears to be a need for more timely action with respect to imports from NMEs. This is due to the surprise factor caused by information gaps occurring between market and nonmarket economies and also within the market economy, where decision making is typically dispersed.

Second, the question of the duration of the safeguard action is not readily limited to a set number of years when dealing with the NMEs. Since the disruption would not be as a result of market forces, which can be expected to work themselves out with adjustments and counteradjustments over time, the safeguard action ideally should be tied to the period of disruption. However, since the absence of a termination date tends to perpetuate safeguard actions, the period could be presumed to be three years unless negotiated by both parties for a shorter period. This type of negotiation would offer the importing country a chance to reduce the period of the safeguard action in return for the efforts of the NME government to withdraw, reduce, or hold constant the offending exports.

Another issue connected with safeguard actions is that of domestic adjustment assistance. Western economic theory holds that under free-market conditions increased imports from a more efficient producer should be permitted. Economic benefits in this case would go to the consumer. Political reality, however, has a way of intruding on economic theory. Domestic adjustment assistance for workers, firms, industries, or regions affected by the increased imports may be necessary to ease and speed up the shift of resources into more productive activities. In dealing with an NME it is difficult to ascertain whether or not the laws of comparative advantage apply. Is the NME product produced more efficiently, or does it merely appear so because of the irrational price structure of the NMEs? For this reason, domestic adjustment assistance may not be as desirable a policy as in cases where the comparative advantages are more clear-cut. In fact, the Trade Act of 1974 precludes its use in the case of market disruption by NMEs.

Finally, in all safeguard actions there is a need for surveillance not currently provided by the GATT articles. That this should be a multilateral surveillance system is necessitated by the fact that safeguard actions often have an adverse impact on third-country markets. Moreover, there is a need for surveillance and for consultations to see that safeguard actions are appropriate to the amount of disruption caused; if they are not, that any retaliation is justified and appropriate; that the restrictive measures are withdrawn when the market disruption ceases; and that adjustment assistance results in the desired shift in resources, rather than in the entrenchment of an inefficient producer or industry.

In sum, the safeguard actions in the case of NMEs should permit differing injury criteria and non-MFN application, and should be swift, potentially short term, and not necessarily linked to domestic adjustment measures.[8] Nevertheless, domestic adjustment policies, while perhaps not as necessary in NME cases, should not be completely precluded—especially with regard to instances where long-term, nonstrategic comparative advantage can be determined—for reasons of economic efficiency and reduced costs to consumers.

In the final analysis the logic of the market system, which neatly distinguishes between safeguards and antidumping and countervailing actions, breaks down when applied to nonmarket economies. This is why U.S. policymakers have resorted to the concept of market disruption in dealing with the NMEs. A market disruption approach is probably the best solution currently available, short of negotiating an unfair trade practices code with the NMEs. Aside from questions about the desirability of such a code, such an event is not likely to occur in the near future, if at all. The problem with the market disruption approach, of course, is that it is more likely to fall prey to protectionist manipulation.

With regard to the MTN it seems unlikely that the injury criteria for the escape clause will be revised either as between Western nations or in such a way as to establish a different criterion for the NMEs. However, it may be possible to revise the current interpretation that safeguard actions must be taken on an MFN basis, to improve the procedures for consultation, and to establish some form of continued surveillance, all of which reforms would be helpful in safeguard actions taken against NME GATT members. Nevertheless, it would also be useful to be able to take safeguard actions more readily against NMEs and at the same time make it more difficult to invoke antidumping or countervailing duties against them.

In public discussion the Eastern Europeans and Soviets have traditionally rejected any differential status. They have in fact accepted de facto discrimination where necessary in order to permit trade to occur. On its part, the West will continue to require effective protection. It might well be in the interest of the NMEs to see a revised and effective safeguard system supersede such practices as quantitative restrictions, discriminatory application of antidumping and countervailing regulations, and other nontariff barriers.

Quantitative Restrictions

Of all the barriers to trade, the various quantitative restrictions (QRs) maintained against the Eastern European nations are the most onerous barriers (short of the outright denial of MFN status) and the most important issue for the NMEs in the MTN. The continuation of QRs was negotiated in the GATT accession agreements of Poland, Hungary, and Romania, and progress has been slight in their liberalization. As of 1974, 59 percent (compared with a 1969 figure of 40 percent) of 1,097 EC list items had been liberalized vis-à-vis NMEs, as against 84 percent for GATT countries as a whole.[9] Austria and the European Community have maintained the largest number of restrictions, although in 1975 Austria removed its QRs on industrial products. The NMEs regard QRs as their largest problem, and all three NMEs most affected—Poland, Romania, and Hungary—have representatives on the QR subgroup.

Bilateral and multilateral consultations on the reduction of QRs have begun, but progress has been halting. It has been agreed in principle—and only after much discussion between the United States and the European Community—to discuss agricultural quantitative restrictions, where some of the most difficult and persistent QRs exist, in both the QR and the agriculture subgroups. Draft codes for licensing (to eliminate licensing for statistical reporting reasons, and to simplify licensing procedures for the administration of quotas) are on the table for discussion. In general, NME licensing procedures are administered for the purpose of documenting exports and imports and, like their Western counterparts, can but need not be used to bureaucratically impede the flow of trade. They will therefore not be discussed here.

While direct quantitative restrictions (lists of prohibited or restricted imports) are not, strictly speaking, NME trade policy instruments, monopolies functioning as buying and selling agents according to a strict central plan provide the same effect as QRs. In a state trading country, imports can be brought in only by an affirmative decision. The planning document itself may thus constitute a schedule of QRs or specified imports.

The lack of an exact counterpart might, to some extent, argue against the removal of discriminatory QRs from the NMEs. However, within the context of the Western trading system, QRs are some of the more damaging and least flexible of protective trade measures in use. QRs which employ ceilings below the domestic demand for an imported product can severely limit or even block the importation of that product. This subsidizes the less efficient domestic producers, raises costs to consumers, and reduces the choices available to consumers. Unlike a tariff, a quota generates no revenues for the government (in fact, it can be quite costly to administer) but returns all the economic benefits to the domestic producers, at the expense of the consumer sector.[10] Even in the absence of reciprocity from the NMEs, reduction of QRs should be attempted for reasons of their disruptiveness alone. Reciprocity should not be sought at the price of abandoning efficient trade concepts altogether. It is interesting to contrast the effects of quota systems with those of market disruption systems. Under market disruption actions, fines or penalties (such as antidumping or countervailing duties) would act like tariffs. Restraints or limitations (such as impounding products subject to an antidumping inquiry, or voluntary export restraints on the part of the NME) would act like quotas. While extensive quota systems can be highly disruptive, an active application of market disruption actions using quantitative limitations can have much the same effect. When this occurs, the need for protection should be carefully weighed against the economic cost of that protection.

Agriculture

The NMEs have an interest in eliminating some of the many QRs on agricultural products imposed by most nations of the world. The MTN agriculture subgroups on grains, dairy products, and meat are at work. Agriculture is perhaps the most difficult area (due to the extreme politicization of issues between the United States and the European Community that has gone on since the Kennedy Round) in which to predict the degree of possible success. One can say, however, that the NMEs have a considerable amount to gain from liberalization on meats and, to a lesser extent, dairy products.

Further, the possibility of a multilateral grains agreement introduces the interesting question of participation by the Soviet Union. While the Soviet Union's participation the MTN is an unlikely proposition, there is some interest (although it is by no means universal) in the West in encouraging the USSR to participate in a grains agreement. Despite the fact that the Soviet Union has concluded a long-term grains agreement with the United States, it is clear that any multilateral agreement relating to grains would be impaired without the USSR because of the magnitude of its purchases. Given the political problems and uncertainty of supply, it would be in the Soviets' interest to participate. Participation by the USSR in a multilateral grains agreement would be an interesting step in the direction of its participation in the multilateral trading system.

Tariffs

Because of the nature of their economic system, tariffs have little impact on the decision of NME countries to purchase an import. Therefore a reduction or increase of tariffs by NMEs has little impact on trade flows, and does not constitute a concession which is equivalent to the reduction of a tariff by a market economy, where price is often the critical variable. However, the effect of NME tariffs varies from country to country. Hungary, for example, has a tariff system which does affect the decision to import due to the fact that the foreign trade organization and planning is decentralized to a considerable degree. In Hungary's accession to GATT, its tariff was accepted as a basis for reciprocal concessions. Poland and Romania have newly established tariff systems. Most Western observers, however, are well aware of the limitations of such tariffs in the absence of a decentralized foreign trade sector, and will no doubt adopt a wait-and-see attitude about their effectiveness as well as demand other concessions to insure reciprocity. What tariff liberalization does occur in the MTN will be of benefit to the NMEs and should increase their exports and their supply of hard currency. The gains could be considerable if linked with significant liberalization in QRs.

There has been much discussion about seeking sector-specific import commitments on the part of the NMEs as reciprocal commitments to tariff liberalization, i.e., commitments to increase imports of specific sectors of special interest to the West, say, for example, specialty steels. Sectoral import commitments fall prey to much the same criticism as general import commitments. Gains can be met through inflation or through increased trade with CMEA partners who are GATT members. Obtaining an increased import commitment in a sector that would probably have been expanded anyway is obviously no real concession. Under these circumstances, and postulating continued inflation, increased sectoral import commitments could amount to little more than one-time deficiency payments. Inasmuch as particular gains can be obtained in this fashion, and effective reciprocity obtained for tariff reductions, sectoral import commitments are useful and significantly better than unilateral trade liberalization, particularly if agreements can be reached which would affect revisions of the current set of five-year plans and the drafting of the next set of five-year plans. However, sectoral import commitments do not attempt to accommodate any of the structural differences which are the root cause of problems of reciprocity in East-West trade.

Conclusions and Recommendations

Related Issues

Several related issues have not yet been discussed, and they will be briefly reviewed here. The problems dividing the United States and the European Community (EC) could prove to be a major stumbling block in the negotiations and could have some spillover into East-West issues. As a matter of fact, East-West issues are not high on the EC priority list for the MTN. Community members are much more concerned about their differences with the United States. East-West trade is something they have engaged in for some time relatively smoothly, and the largest institutional issue for the EC is establishing itself with the Eastern European nations as the negotiating authority in place of the former system of individual bilateral trade agreements. Further, most of the Western Europeans have not had the same heated internal debates over the conditions of East-West trade that occurred in the United States. The EC is more concerned about protection from Asian imports. Finally, in terms of general trade issues, the EC is more interested in tariffs than in nontariff barriers.

The quantitative restrictions issue in the MTN discussions is a sensitive one. The Eastern Europeans are of course interested in the liberalization of QRs, but the EC in general has taken the position that QRs have already been greatly liberalized. The EC may wish to negotiate the liberalization of QRs when it renegotiates a common external trade policy with the nonmarket economies, rather than to do so in the MTN. Further, the European Community wants agricultural QRs to be discussed in the agriculture group, while the United States feels that they should be discussed in the QR subgroup. The debate revolving around agricultural issues has been acrimonious and has focused on procedures rather than substance, a standard negotiating tactic when negotiators are far apart on substantive matters. General success or failure on other agricultural issues could affect the ability of the United States and the Eastern Europeans to achieve a meaningful reduction in QRs.

Intra-CMEA relations will also have an impact on the negotiations. Their positions will be more consistent, since their interests are more homogeneous. They may, in several instances, choose to align themselves with the developing nations for ideological reasons, although there are also strong forces working in the opposite direction, for instance, the desire of such countries as Czechoslovakia, Hungary, and Poland to be regarded as industrialized nations. Another issue is the degree and extent of Soviet participation. So far, the Soviets have followed the issues closely and have monitored the progress of the negotiations. They have not indicated any formal interest in participation in the MTN itself. However, it is highly desirable that they join the grains agreement, and to a lesser extent the standards code.

There is also the question, thus far avoided, of MFN status and the possibility of change in the current U.S. legislation which would permit the granting of MFN status to those countries not now eligible. Should this unlikely event occur, the bargaining position of the United States with the NMEs would be strengthened by a quantum jump, as would the interest of the NMEs in cooperating with the West to create a trading system which functions more equitably for both groups of nations. Conversely, if MFN status is not granted agreements reached in tariff negotiations will not apply between the United States and those nations to whom it denies MFN status, and in all likelihood less will be negotiated on nontariff barriers than might otherwise be possible.

Western Interests vis-à-vis the East in the MTN

A ranking of Western interests at the MTN is presented in table V-1. Primarily, the West will be interested in obtaining some measure of effective reciprocity for reductions in tariffs and QRs. The problem is that under the GATT system no ready categories present themselves. A better safeguard system is needed, but revisions of the safeguard system may not be undertaken with East-West issues in mind. The heart of the problem of reciprocity lies in the area of NME planning, foreign trade organization, industrial organization, market access, and domestic prices. The ability to negotiate these matters in a multilateral forum is not even a remote possibility. This is not to say that efforts should not be made to seek means of accommodation and, where possible, to promote multilateral approaches. But in the absence of even rudimentary accommodation agreements, commitments to increase imports in critical sectors will have to continue to be used, despite their disadvantages.

Given these conditions, there are two ways to view the MTN. In the first perspective, the West will be granting tariff and other concessions for which only partial reciprocity is possible. The second way of viewing the negotiations is that at least a significant amount of discussion about reform will take place, especially with regard to nontariff barriers. In each instance, there is the opportunity to consider the nonmarket context. A series of codes may well emerge from the deliberations, which will involve varying participants, some of them NMEs. The object of such an ad hoc and pragmatic approach would be to develop an array of rules that apply to transactions between the two types of economies without attempting to create a new East-West mechanism or a new set of articles to the GATT, approaches which at best are premature.

Eastern Interests vis-à-vis the West in the MTN

The main Eastern interests in the MTN are to have their tariffs accepted and to reduce the extent of QRs maintained against their products. The Eastern European nations will also be interested in easing the arbitrary effects of antidumping and countervailing duties. They will no doubt be interested in minimizing Soviet influence on the negotiations and on their trade patterns generally. They will benefit, as will other nations, from the tariff reductions agreed upon. They will participate in the MTN more actively than in past GATT negotiations. It is definitely in the interest of the Eastern Europeans to participate in the MTN, both because of real benefits and because of the inability of that particular forum to obtain full reciprocity from NMEs.

On the negative side, they will probably receive less than full recognition for their tariffs, and no doubt the most troublesome QRs will remain untouched. They may have to accept on a case-by-case basis some differences in the applicability of rules, such as countervailing duties and safeguards. For those who do not already enjoy it, MFN status cannot be granted by the United States via multilaterals. (See table V-1 for a listing of issues of priority to the East in the MTN.)

Recommendations for the MTN

What should be the goals of the MTN in the context of East-West trade? These will necessarily be modest—but not unimportant. This paper has attempted to discuss the full range of issues that will be raised in the MTN which have some application to problems of East-West trade. As negotiations go, it cannot be expected that all issues under discussion in the MTN will be concluded successfully. Progress on East-West issues will no doubt be even more circumscribed. Nevertheless, one can ask what the MTN can reasonably be expected to achieve, and where significant effort should be applied in order to make progress.

The MTN can accomplish—

- negotiation of a standards code with NME participation
- reduction of QRs
- reduction, liberalization and harmonization of tariffs generally

The negotiations should attempt to introduce and address East-West issues; for example, they should—

- explore informally issues of comparability in subsidization practices
- consider NME price structure to more fairly evaluate antidumping cases

Table V-1
EAST-WEST TRADE PROBLEM AREAS:
PRIORITIES IN THE MTN

	MTN Priority	
Practice	To West	To East
Harmful/discriminatory to West:		
1. Government purchasing policies	Low	Nil
2. Subsidization (general & export)	Moderate/Low	Nil
3. Tariff systems	High	High
4. Centralized decision-making (planning)	Low	Nil
5. Information issues	Low	Low
Harmful/discriminatory to East:		
1. Lack of MFN [(a)]	Nil	Low
2. Quantitative restrictions	Moderate	High
3. Safeguards	High	Low
4. Market-oriented rules (anti-dumping, countervailing)	Low	High
Relatively mutual:		
1. Standards	High	Moderate

Ordering by mutual priorities:
1. Tariffs
2. Standards, quantitative restrictions
3. Safeguards and market oriented rules (anti-dumping & countervailing)
4. Information issues and subsidization
5. All others: government purchasing, centralized decisionmaking, lack of MFN.

(a) The lack of MFN will not be directly addressed in the MTN and is therefore of low priority in this context. It is not of low priority in any other context.

consider a single market disruption test for NMEs
negotiate sectoral import commitments

Reciprocity

On balance, given the high degree of structural asymmetry caused by the differing economic and political systems, it is remarkable that trade occurs to the degree that it does. The reason that it not only occurs but is increasing is that, all in all, the West can rely on rather effective protection measures to offset other disadvantages. And the East benefits by participation even though the rules of the game are not entirely "fair," from its perspective. Were there no mutual advantages, obviously trade would not occur at all.

Where then does reciprocity lie? Given the difficulty of the subject, it is better to start with the negative. First, it cannot be obtained in the context of any one issue, but must reflect the totality. (Table V-2 approaches the question of reciprocity by assessing the mutuality/asymmetry factors in the issues which will come up in the MTN, but makes no assessment of the relative impact of each problem area on East-West trade.) Second, it cannot exist today, given the current institutional and structural asymmetries and the absence of serious efforts to accommodate these differences. Third, in the absence of an effective multilateral institutional mechanism that can accommodate the two systems, the bilateral trade agreement remains the most important mechanism for attempting to obtain reciprocity. The preeminent role of the bilateral agreement in East-West trade would be likely to continue even if multilateral institutions could be improved.

In reality, then, reciprocity can only be assessed when bilateral arrangements, multilateral institutions and codes, business facilitation agreements, tariff issues, nontariff issues, and safeguards are all considered. A group of both Western and Eastern experts concluded that in seeking to expand trade it was necessary to consider "not only tariffs and the discrimination which might exist in this regard but also other forms of State policy determining access to markets, and to seek to attain equality of treatment on the basis of undertakings which would have mutually advantageous and equivalent trade effects in both types of economy."[11] Reciprocity may not be just around the corner, but progress is possible, and it is movement in a forward direction that should be sought.

Table V-2
MUTUALITY FACTORS IN MTN ISSUES

Issue	Pro-Western Aspects	Pro-Eastern Aspects	Mutuality
1. Standards	Voluntary—requires best efforts; government mandatory	Easier to institute & administer	High degree
2. QRs	Very effective, highly protective	Central plan for imports has a similar effect	None
3. Tariffs	Denial of MFN	Non-parallel function	Some, varies from country to country and item by item
4. Safeguards	Useful protection—insurance and deterrent functions	Necessary to maintain relationship	None
5. Anti-dumping rules	Market-oriented pricing	Can stimulate improved marketing	None
6. Subsidies	Countervailing duty regulation and construction	Pervasiveness & extent Lack of applicability to GATT provisions	Degree to which Western nations subsidize

Summary:
1. Standards: High degree of mutuality/some asymmetry (neutral)
2. QRs: High degree of asymmetry/little mutuality (pro-West); effect of central plan (pro-East)
3. Tariffs: High degree of asymmetry/some mutuality (pro-East)
4. Safeguards: High degree of asymmetry/little mutuality (pro-West)
5. Anti-dumping rules: High degree of asymmetry/little mutuality (pro-West)
6. Subsidies: High degree of asymmetry/some mutuality (pro-East)

For the time being, bilateral agreements between market and nonmarket economies are the most workable accommodation mechanisms available. However, as East-West trade increases, the need for multilateral harmonization will also increase. Against such a backdrop, the negotiations being held in Geneva can be most useful in bringing to light and discussing specific problem areas (rather than general commitments). An indicator of the success of MTN in the field of East-West trade would be the continuation of such specific East-West discussions after the final agreements have been signed and the negotiators have left Geneva.

What Type of Trading System for the Future?

The present GATT system has undergone a high degree of evolution. There is a difference of opinion whether the change has been beneficial or not. However, even considering the amount of alteration that has occurred, it is not likely that either a single new set of articles governing relations between nonmarket and market economies could be negotiated now or in the future, or that such an agreement could be negotiated outside of the GATT. These alternatives are probably not acceptable either to the GATT countries or the NMEs.

What does seem to be possible in the future is a series of codes and special regulations dealing with specific issues and affiliated with the GATT structure. Special protocols could be added in each instance describing the special criteria, rules, and regulations which would apply in a market/nonmarket context for that particular code. The codes would be open to membership by all nations, but benefits would apply only to members. This would seem to be a practical way to reduce the differences which separate the market and nonmarket countries.

However, there is an important problem with this scenario. It would be possible for a country to join several or all of the codes without ever taking on the greater GATT responsibilities that were carefully enumerated by its drafters in an attempt to maximize the efficiency of the trading system and minimize the degree of political intervention in economic affairs. Most, if not all, of what might be lost under such circumstances could be protected in bilateral arrangements. However, the valid question remains how to induce a country to take the final step and make a commitment to at least the minimum elements of rights and obligations that the GATT system provides.

The other remaining question is whether it is advantageous to try to improve the degree of multilateralism in East-West trade. Such trade is continuing to grow, despite some severe restraints on both sides. Organizational and institutional trade reform issues are academic unless there is the necessary political will and economic advantage to increase trade. But if stabilization, harmonization, and steady expansion are valid objectives, then these would be advanced by increasing the amount of trade that is subject to mutually agreed rules and institutions.

6

Financing U.S. Exports to the Soviet Union and Eastern Europe

Alfred R. Wentworth

The Emergence of the Soviet Union and Eastern Europe as a Significant Market

The emergence of the Soviet Union and Eastern Europe[1] as markets for countries exporting capital goods and technology is relatively recent, and it is important that the United States be competitive at this critical time. For instance, once a Swedish or a French airways control system is in place in one of these countries, new orders for modernization, replacement, or expansion almost automatically flow to the original supplier. While the United States may deny the importing country normal trade relationships on grounds that the country does not meet our notion of adequate internal freedom for individuals, other exporting countries have not been as moralistic as we, and as a result are attaining competitive commercial advantage over the United States. Concrete examples of the desire to capture the Soviet market are recent lines of credit extended by other countries to the USSR: the $1.95 billion worth of export credit from Britain, $2.8 billion from France, and $500 million from Canada. Before further American loans were blocked by the 1974 Trade Act, our Eximbank had authorized credits (outstanding loans or unused commitments) of only $470 million, and the Export-Import Bank Act limited new credits to an additional $300 million. The severe limitations on Eximbank credit to the Soviet Union have been justified by the Congress not on the Soviet Union's credit standing, but on a desire by Congress to achieve greater supervision over the affairs of the Export-Import Bank and over the foreign policy implications of its actions.

The compelling argument for the United States to improve its East-West trade financing capacity today is competitiveness. American business firms are encountering stiff Western European and Japanese competition in numerous areas, including computers, machine tools, shipping, chemical engineering, and automotive equipment. In many cases, foreign countries have technologies and products for sale which are comparable to American ones, and have adequate financing as well. The USSR, as mentioned above, has ample credit available from government sources in both Western Europe and Japan.

Soviet Union and Eastern European Credit Standing and Repayments Prospects

Certainly the U.S. private banking industry considers that Soviet and other Eastern European countries' credit standing remains excellent. This view is based on judgmental factors, but also most importantly on information published in both Western and Eastern Europe. The Soviet Union is the second largest economy in the world, and in terms of GNP Eastern Europe equals the size of the European Community. It is only very recently that Eastern European countries have entered the world's credit markets in any volume. Their estimated aggregate debt to the West at the end of 1975 totaled about $32 billion, of which the Soviet Union accounted for about $11 billion. Eastern Europe's reserves total some $7.0 billion in foreign exchange, and its gold holdings are estimated to exceed $10 billion. Eastern Europe's total exports to the West are estimated at over $30 billion in 1975. It is the judgment of the financial community that Eastern Europe's foreign debt is manageable. Because much of the foreign exchange debt finances large projects in the Soviet Union, the structure of the debt lends itself to repayment over time from exports generated by these projects.

Compensation Agreements

In connection with large projects the Soviets have devised a technique which they term "compensation agreements." These agreements are the result of the negotiation of two separate and unlinked contracts. The first contract covers the supply of a large plant from a foreign country to the Soviet Union and provides for payment over a period of time. The second contract, usually between the same foreign supplier and the same Soviet ministry or foreign trade organization (FTO), covers the sale of a portion of the product from the plant being supplied, or the sale of some other product, to the foreign supplier of the plant or to another foreign purchaser of the product. This contract is expressed in foreign exchange, with the price to be negotiated annually. Normally the result of this second contract will be sales over time in foreign exchange approximately equal to the cost of the plant. Most importantly, however, the Soviet Union's promise to pay for the plant is unconditional and does not depend on the successful annual negotiation of the second contract.

In its purest form there are multiple advantages to both buyer and seller under such an agreement. The following case, in which an accord was never reached, could be defined as a "pure" agreement, and seemed for a time to stir considerable interest on both sides. The Soviets requested a number of large U.S. construction firms to enter bids for the design and construction on a turnkey basis of a large petroleum refinery north of Moscow. The refinery was to incorporate the latest technology in the field. Further, the bids for the construction contract were to be accompanied by the agreement of a reputable user of refined petroleum products to purchase such products over a period of years at an annually negotiated price to be based on world prices.

Compensation agreements such as the one mentioned

above have the following advantages, among others, to the Soviet buyer:

1. The approval of the plant, both at the ministerial level and at the level of Gosplan, is much easier.
2. Foreign exchange earnings geared to repayment requirements are identified.
3. The Soviets receive assurances that their production will gain acceptance in the West through assured markets there.
4. Contracts to sell products at annually negotiated prices provide a hedge against Western inflation.

Advantages from the Western supplier's point of view are:

1. The construction firm obtains a profitable contract.
2. The exporting countries of the capital goods obtain valuable export markets.
3. The sale of the advanced technology helps the exporting country to pay for research and development costs.
4. The West obtains energy at world prices—a commodity in short supply, and for which diversification of source is urgently needed.

The pricing of the "buy-back" product is vital to the profitability of compensation agreements. One of the most interesting and most practical papers done on the subject advocates that the Western purchaser of Eastern European products agrees to pay the supplier only the cost of production of the product in the West. In other words, if the selling price in the West is made up of cost of production plus sales costs and overhead, the Western buyer should pay the Eastern supplier only the buyer's own cost of production of that product at that time. One such agreement has been reached, it can be said that the Western producer of a product can look upon the Eastern product as an additional source of supply without additional dollar investment for capital equipment.

The Crucial Role of the Export-Import Bank

The ability of the United States to get its fair share of the markets in the USSR and Eastern Europe will depend critically on the availability and competitiveness of U.S. source financing. These, in turn, depend upon aggressive use of Export-Import Bank credit.

Some critics have opposed Export-Import Bank credit to the Soviet Union on the grounds that the USSR has no need for credit and can well afford to pay cash for its imports. The events of 1975, with the harvest shortfall and the subsequent requirement for renewed imports of huge amounts of food and feed grains, point out the need of the USSR for well-structured credit, at least for the portion of their imports representing capital goods. The use of credit for the purchases of capital goods is standard practice in international trade, whether among industrial countries or by countries without much in the way of capital resources. The same logic should apply to such purchases by the USSR. Export-Import Bank credit will accomplish a number of important objectives but will probably not lower interest costs significantly to the borrower.

The United States has taken the initiative, in conjunction with other capital-goods-exporting nations, to standardize credit terms and to reduce or eliminate interest rate subsidies in export credits. Eximbank credit would accomplish a number of things that would make our exports more competitive in the world market structure and make more private financing available for transactions with the USSR and Eastern Europe.

1. Eximbank's participation permits repayment of borrowings over longer periods of time, since Eximbank programs are designed to take the later maturities. Normally the commercial banks extend financing for five to seven years, and Eximbank will go as far as ten to twelve years.
2. The security behind the commercial bank portion of the credit is improved because the Eximbank takes a position subordinate to the commercial banks, receiving no principal repayment until the commercial bank has been completely repaid.
3. The participation of Eximbank in the financing of any export gives automatic exemption from the restrictions

imposed by the Johnson Debt Default Act.[2]

4. The participation of Eximbank also permits the activation of Pefco (The Private Export Funding Corporation), which was formed some five years ago by U.S. commercial banks, investment banks, and exporters of capital equipment from the United States. Pefco, under the overall guarantee of Eximbank, raises its own funds in the market in very large blocks. With these funds, in participation with commercial banks and the Eximbank, Pefco finances the exports of so-called big ticket items, that is, transactions ranging from $50 million and up. Pefco's participation in the many large projects envisioned in the USSR will be vital to the U.S. banking community's ability to finance them. Again, however, Eximbank must have the ability to guarantee Soviet credit risks before Pefco can assist in the financing process.

Private U.S. Banking Resources

Government-backed private U.S. banking resources help considerably to overcome the limiting effect of U.S. banking regulations, which prohibit U.S. commercial banks from lending more than 10 percent of their paid-up capital, reserves, and undivided profit to any one borrower. Up to the present time the Soviet Union has designated only one borrower of bank credit, the Bank for Foreign Trade. A similar situation exists in most other Eastern European countries. There is an aggregate of slightly in excess of $2 billion in total legal limits in the commercial banking system in the United States. The result, in the case of the Soviet Union, is that funds available in the private banking sector (as of June 1976) to finance exports to the USSR may be as little as $600 million. (At the end of 1975 there was about $1 billion in outstanding loans and some $200 million additional in credit commitments to the Soviet Union in the U.S. banking system; this leaves some $800 to $900 million of leeway in the aggregate. However, presumably not all banks would be willing to lend to their legal limit to the Soviet

Union; hence the lower figure seems closer to a practical limit.) When U.S. credit becomes restricted by legal limit inhibitions such as these, the Soviet Union would still be able to nominate additional borrowers and qualify them with U.S. authorities as additional legal limit borrowers. To date, however, this has not been done.

Some questions have been raised as to whether lending to borrowers other than the Bank for Foreign Trade would be prudent on the part of Western bankers, because of fears that lending to borrowers other than the Bank for Foreign Trade would reduce central control over the creation of external liabilities and thus impair the value of repayment guarantees. With a more complete understanding of the functioning of the planning process in the Soviet Union and Eastern Europe such doubts are allayed. There is, in fact, some doubt that the guarantee of the Bank for Foreign Trade adds to the security of the notes of an FTO. Each FTO operates under its annual plan and this plan specifies the foreign exchange to be earned and the foreign exchange liabilities permitted to be created. Each FTO must operate according to its plan and each plan bears the approval, among others, of the Ministry of Finance, the custodian of the country's foreign exchange, and the Ministry of Foreign Trade. The Bank for Foreign Trade functions only as the accumulator and dispenser of foreign exchange in accordance with the over-all plan. It is hoped by Western bankers that eventually the Bank for Foreign Trade could assume the position of the Bank of England or the Bank of Japan, which do not act as guarantors of foreign liability but as entities involved in the regulation of payment of receipts of foreign exchange. In a specific future instance, for example, the Bank of Foreign Trade could state, in response to an inquiry, that a contemplated indebtedness of an FTO was within the plan and, therefore, foreign exchange would be available for repayment of the debt incurred. A statement such as this coupled with increased knowledge of the FTO itself and its financial background would, it is believed, be satisfactory to Western bankers and to the U.S. controller of the currency, thereby establishing additional legal limit borrowers.

Another restraint on U.S. commercial bank lending to Eastern Europe and the USSR has been the lack of customary information on the uses of borrowings, balance of trade, foreign exchange reserves, and debt position and structure in these countries. The one exception is Poland, which has accommodated the international banking community by releasing considerable project information. Other countries may eventually follow suit. As the socialist countries discern a reluctance on the part of lenders in other countries to extend further credit without additional information, it is my belief that pragmatism will prevail and the information will be forthcoming.

Structural Problems in Dealing with the Socialist Banking System

The socialist system has its built-in inhibitions and rigidities that will demand ingenuity from both sides if East-West trade is to develop satisfactorily. As an example, in the Soviet Union only the Bank for Foreign Trade is authorized to negotiate credit from banks abroad, as mentioned earlier. In the recent past, the Bank for Foreign Trade has not been negotiating loans for the import of capital goods, but rather "financial credits" in the Eurodollar market without designation as to particular projects.

Finance for the importation of specific capital goods for projects has been arranged under what the Soviets term "commercial credit," that is, a credit arranged between the importing FTO and the foreign supplier. These negotiations result in the issuance of serial notes of the FTO in favor of the seller. These notes, to be bankable in the West, have up to the present time had to bear the guarantee of the Bank for Foreign Trade. Without information on the FTO obligor sufficient to permit U.S. banks to regard the FTO as a bona fide separate borrower, the guarantee of the Bank for Foreign Trade forces this FTO debt to be included in the legal limit of the Bank for Foreign Trade. Further, the notes generated in "commercial credit" bear interest at 6½ percent to 7 percent. Since there is no market for fixed rate lending available at this low rate, the American seller must build into his price sufficient additional funds so that he can augment the interest rate to conform to the level required by his U.S. bank. All this results in the Soviets' paying an effective interest rate up to about 14 percent fixed.

East-West Bank Office Interchange

In the areas of banking and finance there has been a noticeable trend toward the establishment of representative offices of Western banks in Eastern Europe. This development is a relatively new one, dating from 1972-73. U.S. banks have opened such offices with some hesitation and in a rather restricted manner because of their cost of maintenance, coupled with the relatively low level of trade exchanged. Western European banks have proliferated more quickly and widely, because their trade with Eastern Europe is much more important (see Annex C, table VI-1). Both Western European and U.S. banks open offices in Eastern Europe for roughly the same purposes:

1. Most importantly, such offices function as a channel for information and communication between Western and Eastern businessmen. In the case of the USSR, the banks were perceived by the Soviets as a means of implementing détente and increasing trade with the West. The offices in Eastern Europe give guidance with respect to effective approaches to Eastern markets and to negotiating Eastern European transactions. They also give guidance relating to the structure of the transactions, to assure that they are bankable.
2. Many, although not all, of the offices serve as negotiators of financial credits to the Soviet Union. In all cases they serve as listening posts to pick up information about new financings coming to the market.
3. These offices help their Eastern European host countries to increase exports to the West through market intelligence and information about price, design, and related matters.

4. The offices also serve as interpreters to their Eastern European hosts of significant political and economic developments in the West.

The arrival of Eastern European banking offices in Western Europe has a much longer history, dating from the Moscow Narodny Bank in London in 1919 and the Banque Commerciale pour l'Europe du Nord in Paris in 1921; such offices have greatly expanded in number with the development of the new relationship between Eastern Europe and the West (see Annex C, table VI-2). These offices in Western Europe are not representative offices but are full-fledged operating banks, for in Western Europe the policy of reciprocity has never been established as it has in the United States and particularly in New York State. (Reciprocity in New York State requires that before a bank from a foreign country may *branch* in New York State the foreign country must permit the opening of a *branch* or an *agency* in the foreign country. Agencies and representative offices may be established in New York State without the requirement for reciprocity.)

The various Eastern European entities in Western Europe serve a number of important purposes; for example:

1. They give the Eastern European countries direct access to Western financial markets.
2. They serve as training grounds for Eastern European bankers engaged in international finance.
3. They serve as windows on the Western financial world, increasing Eastern Europe's knowledge of Western financial markets, their functions, and their current conditions.
4. They also take part in financial syndications and have from time to time assisted materially in completing difficult financing for Eastern European borrowers.

It is expected that this increase in the number of Eastern European entities in Western Europe will continue. Further, it is expected that Eastern European banks will establish presences either by representative offices, agencies, or, in certain limited instances, branches in New York City.

Socialist Banking Institutions

Besides the activities of the individual socialist country banks, there are two international CMEA banks whose operations in East-West trade are growing in importance. The International Bank for Economic Cooperation (IBEC) in Moscow is the clearing bank for the CMEA countries. IBEC was established on the basis of a 1963 agreement by representatives of the governments of Bulgaria, Hungary, the German Democratic Republic, Mongolia, Poland, Romania, the USSR, and Czechoslovakia. Cuba became a member in 1974. The agreement provided for the creation of a multilateral system of settlements and of a collective CMEA currency, the transferable ruble.

IBEC is directed by an international council in which all members have an equal voice. The main activity of IBEC is making international settlements and granting credits in transferable rubles. About 95 percent of these settlements result from intra-CMEA trade.

In addition to multilateral settlements, IBEC also carries out operations in Western convertible currencies and in gold. As an international commercial bank it accepts deposits and accounts, receives and grants credits, finances CMEA imports from the West, and in general contributes to the functioning of East-West trade. IBEC is already a major institution in international finance and will undoubtedly become even more important in the years ahead. The bulk of payments for intra-CMEA trade passes through it, and it is also an important conduit for hard-currency credits from the West to socialist countries. This institution is roughly comparable in its function in the CMEA to the International Monetary Fund in the West.

The second CMEA bank is the International Investment Bank (IIB), also headquartered in Moscow, which began its work on January 1, 1971. The main task of IIB is granting medium and long-term credits to member countries. Such credits are made in transferable rubles and in convertible Western currencies and may run up to 15 years. The IIB grants credits for projects which serve the interests of several

CMEA members. Recently, IIB has helped provide credits for the Orenburg gas condensation plant and for the construction of the $7 billion, 1,700-mile pipeline extending from Orenburg to the Western border of the USSR. While there are many differences between them, some comparison can be drawn between IIB and the World Bank in the West. The USSR owns approximately 38 percent of both of these organizations with the remainder of the shares held by other members countries of CMEA, apportioned on the comparative size of their economies. Each organization has had as chairman a high-ranking Soviet former banker.

Convertibility of Currency

A word also needs to be said about currency convertibility, a problem which comes up naturally in any discussion of East-West banking and finance. Eastern European leaders have indicated that the CMEA intends to widen the scope of functions performed by the transferable ruble and that convertibility is an ultimate goal. The reasons are primarily to increase the effectiveness of the CMEA as an economic organization by facilitating greater trade among the member nations and by developing new forms of cooperation such as joint economic ventures among socialist countries. The lack of convertibility poses a significant barrier to these goals. Trade among CMEA states is still based on principles of bilateral balancing and joint ventures, and specialization agreements are hindered by the difficulties of making cost comparisons and payments without a freely convertible currency unit. Since nearly all East-West commerce is denominated in convertible Western currencies, the lack of convertibility of socialist domestic currencies, or of the transferable ruble, does not act as a hindrance to this trade.

Convertibility as generally understood in the West implies a free access to a country's markets to buy or to sell. This immediately creates a problem for socialist countries, since the allocation of resources is primarily decided by means of plans and not by the market. Various forms of limited convertibility would be possible in the future, e.g., by specifying conditions under which foreigners may have access to domestic socialist markets. It would be necessary, however, for the socialist countries to improve further the quality of goods produced to meet Western buyers' expectations, and also to provide a closer link of foreign and domestic prices so that domestic prices will reflect world market price relations to a greater extent than is true today. Although some progress has been made in this direction, notably by Poland and Hungary, convertibility does not appear likely in the near future. Despite these problems the trend toward greater interdependence between East and West in the areas of banking and finance will continue to encourage efforts by socialist countries to introduce greater flexibility into the CMEA financial system.

The Need To Move Ahead

All the aforementioned factors point to the pressing need to reappraise the U.S. East-West trade strategy. In 1975 the United States earned a balance-of-payments surplus of $12 billion overall and a surplus of $2.1 billion with Eastern Europe (including $1.6 billion with the Soviet Union). This highly favorable surplus can be attributed to the fact that 1975 was a year of recession in the United States which lowered our demand for imported energy and other raw materials and at the same time increased our competitiveness in world markets for the sale of American finished products. As we climb out of that recession, our imports will increase, and we must increase our exports correspondingly in order to pay for them. Many business economists are forecasting that the 1976 trade balance will end up with a deficit of $2 to $4 billion. The United States' overall balance-of-payments surplus with Eastern Europe is encouraging, and other Western countries have also done well on this score. In 1975, with Western Europe also in a recession, Western Germany ran up a surplus with Eastern Europe of $3 billion, and France with its much smaller economy had a surplus of $825 million. Japan earned a trade surplus with Eastern Europe of $700 million. These deficits were paid for by Eastern

Europe by running down their foreign exchange reserves, by the increased sale of gold and other products, and through increased borrowings from abroad. A deputy minister of foreign trade of the USSR has announced that in the absence of Export-Import Bank credit and most-favored-nation treatment for the Soviet Union, contracts totaling $1.6 billion have in 1975 been shifted from U.S. suppliers to foreign suppliers, principally France and Japan. (Some of these contracts undoubtedly went, at least partially, to overseas affiliates of U.S. companies.) Such a shift in the source of supply by the Soviet Union costs the U.S. economy jobs at a time we can ill afford to lose them.

Eastern Europeans claim that their economies are not subject to inflation, nor to recession. While they have had to make other sacrifices to maintain this position, up to now they have been at least partially correct. Their economies should, therefore, provide a fairly constant market for our goods. And their ability to create exports through diversion of goods from the domestic to the export market gives them increased ability to pay for imports. With the participation of the Export-Import Bank, the private credit markets of the United States can finance a sizeable volume of exports to Eastern Europe. So far our denial of Eximbank credit and most-favored-nation treatment seems only to have limited our potential in these markets without any corresponding gain in our vigorous efforts to persuade the USSR to permit increased emigration. Although the issue is subject to dispute, there are many, including this author, who feel that by increasing U.S. trade with the Soviet Union we will have a better chance in the long run of inducing the USSR to increase the human freedoms it allows its people. Concurrently, we will be able to take advantage of a huge new market for our exports, thereby enabling us to help pay our own way in this increasingly interdependent world economy.

ANNEX C

Table VI–1

Representation of Western Banks in Eastern Europe

	Soviet Union
Finland	Kansallis-Osake-Pankki
	Union Bank of Finland
France	Banque de Paris et des Pays-Bas
	Banque Nationale de Paris
	Crédit Lyonnais
	Société Générale
FRG	Commerzbank
	Dresdnerbank
	Deutsche Bank
Iran	Bank Melli Iran
Italy	Banca Commerciale Italiana
	Banco di Roma
	Credito Italiano
Sweden	Svenska Handelsbanken
UK	Barclays Tozer Ltd.
	Lloyd's Bank International
	National Westminster Bank
U.S.	Bank of America
	Chase Manhattan Bank
	Citibank
	Hungary
Austria	Creditanstalt-Bankverein
U.S.	Citibank
	German Democratic Republic
France	Crédit Lyonnais
	Société Générale
Italy	Banca Commerciale Italiana
	Romania
U.S.	Manufacturers Hanover Trust
	Poland
France	Banque Nationale de Paris
Italy	Banca Commerciale Italiana
U.S.	First National Bank of Chicago

Table VI-2

Socialist Banks and Affiliates in the West*

Soviet Union

Bank Russo-Iran
Founded in Teheran in 1923; in 1954 U.S.S.R. assumed complete ownership.
Banque Commerciale pour l'Europe du Nord (Eurobank)
Founded in Paris in 1921.
Donaubank
Founded in Vienna in 1974.
East-West United Bank
Founded in Luxembourg in 1975.
Moscow Narodny Bank, Ltd.
Founded in London in 1919 (branches: Beirut-October 1963; Singapore-November 1971; representative office: Moscow-1975).
Ost-West Handelsbank
Founded in Frankfurt in 1972.
Wozchod Handelsbank
Founded in Zurich in 1966.

Hungary

Central Wechsel und Creditbank
Founded in Vienna in 1918 (now wholly-owned subsidiary of National Bank of Hungary).
Hungarian International Bank, Ltd.
Founded in London in 1973.
National Bank of Hungary
Representative offices in Paris, Zurich, Beirut and Frankfurt.

Bulgaria

Bulgarian Foreign Trade Bank
Representative office in London.
Litexbank SAL (Lebanese International Trade and Exchange Bank)
Beirut—1966, successor to Sogexbank after Bulgaria got 50% interest; representative offices in London and Sofia.
Anglo-Romanian Bank, Ltd.
Founded in London in 1973. £3 million authorized; 50% interest held by the Romanian Bank for Foreign Trade, Barclays International 30%, Manufacturers Hanover 20%.
Banque Franco-Roumaine
Founded in Paris in 1971. Founding capital FF20 million, 50% held by the Romanian Bank for Foreign Trade and 50% by eight French banks.
Egyptian-Romanian Bank
Cairo—1975. 10 million Egyptian sterling charter capital, Egypt contributing 51%.
Romanian Bank for Foreign Trade
Representative offices in Frankfurt, London and Rome.

Czechoslovakia

Ceskoslovenska Obchodni Banka
The Commercial Bank of Czechoslovakia was set up in 1965. Beirut, New Delhi, Belgrade representative offices.
Zivnostenska Banka
Founded in London in 1922.

Table VI-2 (cont'd.)

Poland

Bank Handlowy w Warszawie, S.A.
Representative offices in London and New York.
Centro International Handelsbank
Founded in Vienna in 1973. Bank Handlowy plus each listed below has share in charter capital of 65 million schillings. Kleinwort Benson, Ltd. (London), Banque Occidentale pour l'Industrie et le Commerce (Paris), Banco Popular Espanol (Madrid), Banco Sicilia (Palermo), Bank of Tokyo, Ltd., Bank für Arbeit und Wirtschaft (Vienna).
Handlowy Bank for Middle East SAL
Founded in Beirut in 1974.
Mitteleuropäische Handelsbank, Aq.
Founded in Frankfurt/Main in 1973.
PKO (Polska Kasa Opieki)
Paris office since 1930.

* This list was compiled from *Eastwest Markets, Moscow Narodny Bulletin* and other published sources.

Notes

Notes to Chapter 1

1. The nations included in this study are Bulgaria, Czechoslovakia, the German Democratic Republic, Hungary, Poland, Romania, and the USSR.

2. Yugoslavia has evolved sufficiently from the planning patterns of the other socialist countries that it is not considered a nonmarket economy for the purposes of this study, although it maintains relatively close links with the Council for Mutual Economic Assistance.

3. See also "Conclusions and Recommendations" in this chapter.

4. For a discussion of how the nonmarket economies are organized to conduct foreign trade, see chapter 2 of this book.

5. Poland and Yugoslavia enjoyed MFN treatment prior to the 1974 legislation. Romania negotiated a bilateral trade agreement and has received MFN status under the 1974 Trade Act.

6. For a discussion of the role of Eximbank in East-West trade, see chapter 6 of this book.

7. With the unilateral credit declarations adopted in mid-1976 by the U.S., Canada, France, Germany, Japan, Italy, Belgium, and the U.K., steps have been taken to alleviate this problem by providing standards covering cash payments,

interest rates, repayment terms, and mixed credits. Only time will tell how effective these efforts have been and what their impact on East-West trade will be.

8. The Coordinating Committee is an informal body composed of the NATO countries (except Iceland) and Japan which maintains a mutually agreed list of strategic commodities.

9. For a different viewpoint, see the comment by Philip H. Trezise in Annex A.

10. Section 406 (e)(2) states: "Market disruption exists within a domestic industry whenever imports of an article, like or directly competitive with an article produced by such domestic industry, are increasing rapidly, either absolutely or relatively, so as to be a significant cause of material injury, or threat thereof, to such domestic industry."

11. Both sides have, in effect, carried out many of the provisions of the U.S.-USSR Trade Agreement of 1972 which do not require congressional approval. It is quite likely that the USSR would be ready to put this agreement into effect once the U.S. Congress has made unconditional MFN status and credits possible. For a discussion of the U.S.-USSR agreement, see chapter 3 of this book.

12. For a dissenting viewpoint, see the comment by John W. Evans in Annex A.

13. No assumptions are made here about breaking the OPEC price front, about domestic supply-demand ratios in the USSR, nor about the possible use of fossil-fuel pricing policy by the Soviet Union as leverage in negotiations with Eastern European countries.

14. The same factors apply to other natural resources, such as wood and wood products from the Soviet forestry industry.

15. Romania is currently the only nonmarket-economy country which is a member of the IMF and IBRD.

16. See chapter 6 of this book.

17. The six countries are Bulgaria, Cuba, Czechoslovakia, Hungary, Poland, and Romania. For a discussion of the trade negotiations, see chapter 5 of this book.

18. For a discussion of financing East-West trade, see

chapter 6 of this book.

19. The Chase Manhattan Bank, the Bank of America, and Citibank have offices in Moscow; First National Bank of Chicago has an office in Warsaw; Citibank contemplates a representative office in Budapest; and Manufacturers Hanover Trust Co. has a branch in Bucharest.

20. The countries represented in the OECD are Australia, Austria, Belgium, Canada, Denmark, Finland, France, Germany, Greece, Iceland, Ireland, Italy, Japan, Luxembourg, the Netherlands, New Zealand, Norway, Portugal, Spain, Sweden, Switzerland, Turkey, the United Kingdom, and the United States.

Notes to Chapter 2

1. U.S. Department of Commerce, *Selected Trade and Economic Data of the Centrally Planned Economies* (Washington, D.C., May 1975).

2. J. T. Crawford and John Haberstroh, "Survey of Economic Policy Issues in Eastern Europe: Technology, Trade, and the Consumer," in John P. Hardt, ed., *Reorientation and Commercial Relations of the Economies of Eastern Europe* (Washington, D.C.: Joint Economic Committee of the U.S. Congress, 1974), p. 41ff.

3. Ibid., pp. 41-42.

4. Zbigniew M. Fallenbuchl, "East European Integration: Comecon," in Hardt, ed. *Reorientation and Commercial Relations,* p. 84.

5. John P. Hardt, George C. Holliday, and Young C. Kim, *Western Investment in Communist Economies* (Washington, D.C.: U.S. Senate Committee on Foreign Relations, 1974), pp. 1-3.

6. Central Intelligence Agency, Office of Economic Research, *Handbook of Economic Statistics 1975* (Washington, D.C., August 1975), pp. 54-59.

7. Hardt, Holliday, and Kim, *Western Investment in Communist Economies,* p. 4.

8. U.S. Department of Commerce, *Selected Trade and Economic Data,* p. 11.

9. Ibid., p. 15.

10. Crawford and Haberstroh, "Survey of Economic Policy Issues in Eastern Europe," pp. 38-39.

11. U.S. Department of Commerce, *Selected Trade and Economic Data,* pp. 62-64.

12. U.S. Senate Committee on Foreign Relations, "Soviet Foreign Trade," in Morris Bornstein and Daniel R. Fusfeld, eds., *The Soviet Economy: A Book of Readings* (Homewood, Ill.: Richard D. Irwin, 1966), pp. 242-243.

13. A. Belov, "Vzaimovygodnyye kontakty," *Ekonomicheskaya gazeta,* no. 42 (October 1975), p. 21.

14. A. Belichenko, "Plodotvornaya deyatel'nost': 50-letiye Venshtorgbanka SSSR," *Ekonomicheskaya gazeta,* no. 17 (April 1975), p. 22.

15. Samuel Pisar, *Coexistence and Commerce* (New York: McGraw-Hill Book Co., 1970), pp. 154-160.

16. U.S. Senate Committee on Foreign Relations, "Soviet Foreign Trade," pp. 244-246.

17. Yu. Pekshev, "Vazhnyy faktor mira i sotsial'no-ekonomicheskogo progressa," *Planovoye khozyoystvo,* no. 12 (1974), p. 8.

18. Paul Marer and Egon Neuberger, "Commercial Relations Between the United States and Eastern Europe," in Hardt, ed., *Reorientation and Commercial Relations,* p. 573.

19. Willy Linder, "Hungary," in L.A.D. Dellin and Hermann Gross, eds., *Reforms in the Soviet and Eastern European Economies* (Lexington, Mass.: D. C. Heath, 1972), p. 573.

20. Marer and Neuberger, "Commercial Relations," p. 589.

21. J. Quigly, *The Soviet Foreign Trade Monopoly: Institutions and Laws* (Columbus: Ohio State University Press, 1972), pp. 185-186.

22. Pisar, *Coexistence and Commerce,* p. 150.

23. Adam Zwass, "Monetary Cooperation between East and West," *Soviet and East European Foreign Trade* 10, no. 3-4 (Fall and Winter, 1974-1975):81.

24. A. Stupkiewicz, "Some Problems of Organizing the Foreign Trade Apparatus in Poland," from *Handel Zagra-*

niczny, no. 7 (1974) in *Translations on Eastern Europe: Economic and Industrial Affairs,* no. 1206 (December 20, 1974), p. 16.

25. Zwass, "Monetary Cooperation," pp. 81, 85.

26. Ibid., p. 82.

27. C. D. Rohleder, "Romania," in Dellin and Gross, eds., *Reforms in the Soviet and Eastern European Economies,* p. 119.

28. Zwass, "Monetary Cooperation," p. 85.

29. Rohleder, "Romania," p. 119.

30. Zwass, "Monetary Cooperation," p. 80.

31. Michael Gamarnikow, "Balance Sheet on Economic Reforms," in Hardt, ed., *Reorientation and Commercial Relations,* p. 199.

32. L. A. D. Dellin, "Bulgaria," in Dellin and Gross, eds., *Reforms in the Soviet and Eastern European Economies,* p. 52.

33. Gamarnikow, "Balance Sheet on Economic Reforms," pp. 204-207.

34. Zwass, "Monetary Cooperation," pp. 81-82.

35. Eugene A. Theroux, "Legal and Practical Problems in the China Trade," in *China: A Reassessment of the Economy* (Washington, D.C.: Joint Economic Committee of the U.S. Congress, 1975), pp. 536-543.

36. Bonnie M. Pounds and Mona F. Levine, "Legislative, Institutional, and Negotiating Aspects of United States-Eastern European Trade and Economic Relations," in Hardt, ed., *Reorientation and Commercial Relations,* pp. 548-549.

37. James R. Basche, Jr., *Evolving Corporate Policy and Organization for East-West Trade* (New York: The Conference Board, 1975), p. 3.

38. Basche, *Evolving Corporate Policy and Organization,* pp. 6-7.

39. East-West Foreign Trade Board, *Fourth Quarterly Report* (Washington, D.C., March 1976), pp. 4-6.

40. Pounds and Levine, "Legislative, Institutional, and Negotiating Aspects," pp. 541-543.

41. Ibid.

42. Andrew Elias and Marjory Searing, "A Quantitative Assessment on Trade with Eastern Europe and the USSR," in Hardt, ed., *Reorientation and Commercial Relations*, p. 622.

43. Marer and Neuberger, "Commercial Relations," pp. 570-571.

44. *Nineteenth Annual Report of the President on the Trade Agreements Program—1974* (Washington, D.C., 1975), pp. 46-47.

45. Marer and Neuberger, "Commercial Relations," p. 562.

46. Ibid.

47. Results of the study by T. Wolf are reported in Marer and Neuberger, "Commercial Relations," p. 562.

48. *Nineteenth Annual Report of the President*, pp. 46-47.

49. Elias and Searing, "A Quantitative Assessment on Trade," pp. 606-609.

50. *Nineteenth Annual Report of the President*, pp. 28, 47.

51. East-West Foreign Trade Board, *Fourth Quarterly Report*, p. 8.

52. Elias and Searing, "A Quantitative Assessment on Trade," p. 607.

Notes to Chapter 3

1. Pre-World War II agreements with these countries included the traditional interests of the nation-state: extradition, arbitration, conciliation, postal accords, copyrights, etc. Around World War II there was a series of lend-lease agreements and agreements on national cemeteries. In the 1950s there were virtually no agreements until late in the decade, when a series of agricultural and media guarantee agreements was negotiated with Poland.

2. The Romanian case was quite different. MFN status and the application of GATT obligations followed the bilateral agreement.

3. Peter G. Peterson, U.S. Department of Commerce,

U.S.-Soviet Commercial Relationships in a New Era (Washington, D.C., August 1972), p. 1.

4. Peter G. Peterson, news conference, *Department of State Bulletin,* November 20, 1972, p. 584.

5. The USSR signed the Universal Copyright Convention of 1952 in May 1973, but has not yet signed the revised UCC Agreement of 1971. A tax treaty with the Soviet Union went into effect in January 1976.

6. Statement by Hon. William E. Simon before the U.S. Senate Committee on Commerce, December 11, 1975.

7. It should be remembered that nothing in the Trade Act prohibits the United States from concluding a general bilateral with an MFN country as long as such a bilateral advances the goals of the act.

8. Seweryn Pulawski & Bronislaw Sulimierski, "Trade Exchange and Industrial Cooperation of Poland with the U.S.," *Handel Zagraniczny,* no. 1 (January 1975), pp. 11-15 (in Polish).

9. United Nations, *Economic Bulletin for Europe* 25 (1974), and Harold Horstmeyer, "East-West Trade Expansion Linked to Industrial Cooperation Accords," *New York Journal of Commerce,* October 28, 1975, p. 1A.

10. *Eastern Europe Report* (Business International), November 15, 1974, p. 346.

11. At the same time Valéry Giscard d'Estaing and Leonid Brezhnev also signed a credit agreement on financing major economic cooperation projects to be implemented in the 1975-1979 period; a protocol to the ten-year industrial cooperation program adding several new projects; and an agreement on additional supplies of natural gas for France.

12. The relationship between the FRG and the German Democratic Republic is not examined here because of its highly special nature.

13. The joint commission provided for in each free trade agreement oversees the safeguard action, but in the event of disagreement (the commission functions by mutual consent), or inaction for a period of three months, the injured party can take virtually any action whatsoever.

14. Economic Commission for Europe, *Analytical Report*

on Industrial Cooperation Among ECE Countries (Geneva: United Nations, 1973), p. 2.

15. *East-West Industrial Cooperation Agreements*, report by the International Chamber of Commerce with the Chambers of Commerce of Socialist Countries, ICC doc. no. 555/35, pp. 16-22.

16. H. Peter Dreyer, "EEC States Cling to East Deals," *New York Journal of Commerce*, December 11, 1974.

17. For a discussion of ways to liberalize the treatment of joint venture products, see "The Activities of the UN Economic Commission for Europe in the Field of Industrial Cooperation," note by the ECE Secretariat (Geneva, November 7, 1975), pp. 7-8.

18. For details of the Romanian and Hungarian laws see Bonnie Pounds and Mona Levine, "Legislative, Industrial and Negotiating Aspects of the U.S.-East European Trade and Economic Relations," in *Reorientation and Commercial Relations of the Economies of Eastern Europe*, Joint Economic Committee Compendium (Washington, D.C., August 16, 1974), pp. 550-552.

19. *East-West Markets* (Chase World Information Newsletter), December 15, 1975, p. 6.

20. Thomas A. Wolf, *East-West Economic Relations and the MNC*, Occasional Paper no. 5 of the Center for Multinational Studies (Washington, D.C., July 1973), p. 84.

21. At the time of the U.S.-USSR Agreement, each government agreed to make available to the other, on a reciprocal basis, the usual and customary credit arrangements for the financing of exports. The U.S. determination that a country is eligible to receive Eximbank credits makes no statement to the effect that credits are important to the bilateral relationship or that the U.S. government will facilitate the extension of Eximbank credits.

22. The U.S. Trade Act of 1974 requires that all trade concessions negotiated multilaterally be reciprocated, but presumably a tariff concession to an NME could be reciprocated through the reduction of a nontariff barrier.

23. Excerpts of select market disruption clauses are provided in Annex B.

Notes to Chapter 4

1. *Basic Instruments and Selected Documents* (hereafter referred to as BISD), vol. 1, May 1952, p. 77. BISD is the annual GATT publication incorporating decisions by the contracting parties, reports of working parties, etc.

2. BISD, vol. 2, p. 28.

3. BISD, 8th supplement, 1960, p. 17.

4. Not to be confused with the "provisional application" that applies to all full contracting parties. In GATT terminology, "provisional accession" is the term applied to acceptance of GATT obligations pending the negotiation of the acceding country's tariff schedule.

5. BISD, 11th supplement, 1963, p. 50.

6. Normally, as a condition of accession, a country must negotiate reductions in tariffs. The resulting concessions are bound against increase and incorporated in the country's "schedule."

7. BISD, 15th supplement, 1967, p. 53.

8. BISD, 18th supplement, 1972, p. 201.

9. Article XXXV permits a contracting party, before a new country accedes to the agreement, to decline to enter into GATT relations with it.

10. "Quantitative restrictions . . . inconsistent with Article XIII."

11. "In the case of imports from a country . . . where all domestic prices are fixed by the state . . . a strict comparison [with that country's domestic prices, in order to establish the existence of dumping] may not always be appropriate."

12. For a useful summary of the diplomatic and legislative background, see Stanley Metzger, "Most-Favored-Nation Treatment of Imports to the U.S. from the USSR," *The International Trade Law Journal* 1, no. 1 (Spring 1975): 79-86.

13. For convenience in what follows, the term NME will be understood to exclude these two countries unless their inclusion is clear in the context.

Notes to Chapter 5

1. Of the six countries listed, only Bulgaria is not a GATT member. Bulgaria does have GATT observer status, however. In contrast, at the time of the Kennedy Round only two NMEs participated: Poland and Czechoslovakia. Yugoslavia is participating in the MTN, as it did in the Kennedy Round, but is not considered to be an NME. Of the six currently participating only Poland and Romania receive MFN treatment from the United States.

2. Nontariff barriers are *all* government measures, *other than tariffs,* which impede the flow of trade. This necessarily covers a wide variety of practices, including some that closely resemble tariffs, such as import surcharges, and some that would seem to have little connection with trade, such as regional development programs. The terms "nontariff distortions" and "nontariff measures" are widely used and have approximately the same meaning. The semantic controversies are considerable and will not be detailed here.

3. Discriminatory bilaterals and shipping regulations have been eliminated because they will probably not figure prominently in the negotiations. This does not mean they are unimportant factors in East-West trade. On the contrary, discriminatory bilaterals were the most prevalent form of nontariff barrier cited against the NMEs in the 1974 Tariff Commission study of trade barriers. Government procurement, customs matters, and special duties on imports will be discussed in the MTN but have not been major East-West problems.

4. For a discussion of the problem of defining a subsidy, see U.S. Tariff Commission, *Nontariff Trade Barriers: Report to the Senate Committee on Finance,* pt. 2, vol. 6 (April 1974), pp. 8-10.

5. The practices listed by the 1960 working party, while not exhaustive, "generally are to be considered as subsidies in the sense of Article XVI:4." GATT, *Basic Instruments and Selected Documents: 9th Supplement* (1961), pp. 186-187.

6. European Community, "Aide-Mémoire on the Multilateral Trade Negotiations in GATT," Background Note no. 35/1975 (Washington, D.C.: European Communities Information Service, November 12, 1975).

7. Voluntary export controls or "gentleman's agreements" are agreements on the part of exporters to limit the amount of their products going to the importing nation. These controls are accepted by exporting nations so that they can maintain at least a share of the importing country's market in the face of forceful persuasion by the importing country that safeguard actions or other economic weapons might be employed. The arguments which follow concerning regulating safeguard actions can also be applied to the regulation of voluntary export restraints. The U.S.-USSR Bilateral Trade Agreement of 1972 adopts a "gentleman's agreement" approach to market disruption, i.e., consultations and restraint by the exporter are called for. This raises the question of whether or not voluntary export controls have a special or different role in East-West trade.

8. Most of the above provisions have been incorporated into Section 406 of the 1974 Trade Act.

9. United Nations, *Economic Bulletin for Europe* 25 (1974): 58.

10. None of the above should be construed as a defense of tariffs. Both tariffs and quotas disrupt the benefits derived from trade based on comparative advantage. Tariffs, however, are much easier to detect and their effects are more readily measured.

11. United Nations, Economic Commission for Europe, "Report of Ad Hoc Group of Experts" (E/CONF/46/PC/47), par. 12.

Notes to Chapter 6

1. The term "Eastern Europe" is used in this chapter to cover Bulgaria, Czechoslovakia, East Germany, Hungary, Poland, and Romania; where the context does not indicate otherwise, it also includes the Soviet Union.

2. The Johnson Debt Default Act of 1934 (as amended) prohibits private institutions from extending loans to certain countries (those that are not members of the IMF and World Bank) unless the loans cover U.S. exports and the terms of the credit reflect normal commercial terms.